Murabaha Financing
VS
Lending on Interest

Murabaha Financing VS Lending on Interest

A thin line making big rationale of differentiation

Qazi Irfan
Islamabad (Pakistan)
January 20, 2020

Murabaha Financing VS Lending on Interest
A thin line making big rationale of differentiation
By Qazi Irfan

Cover Art & Design
By Qazi Wahaj

ISBN: 9798601816984

Notice of Rights:

Edition: First

First in book form; a concise article with same title was published on July 22, 2008 and was shared on an Internet forum; it was posted on SSRN website where it is still available. Few thoughts were shortened or withheld then to keep the size of the article short. As expected, the book is more clear and understandable having ample new content.

Author Website:
www.hazariba.com

Author Contact Email:
qazi.irfan.mvl@gmail.com

PREFACE

The origin of query stays more than thousand years back in history; until now, we only have seen financial and legal comparisons but none could ever expose the thin line of economic distinction which actually makes a massive difference in questioned transactions. I was wondering in this desert of mystification and untoward ambiance since early eighties of the previous century, it was quite challenging for me since engineers are not so good in social sciences especially economics, yet by the grace of the Almighty, here is one convincing product of thoughts that may provide concrete foundation for a due change. This is an eye-opener for people in general and to those who are responsible to build institutions and practices in any society. If truth be told, sadly, the current financial practices are posing a colossal threat to societies worldwide because the economics behind is clueless; the previous financial crisis of 2008 was just a glimpse of an expected global financial systems' failure. Though the intuited threat has not hit the world as yet, but if it does or when it does, that might be a universal disaster resulting in never-seen human tragedies. I was self-inclined to explore the possibility of correcting the existing financial methodology or to look for a doable alternative philosophy that may help save the masses from such fiasco. In my view, most long pending issues have fundamental philosophical lapses at the root. The case is not different here too. In this comparison of two transactions, the philosophical lapses of contemporary economic and financial system are exposed clearly. The book will assist unprejudiced minds to figure out what is wrong in current financial system and what shall be there in a corrected or alternative system. The system in place is illegal inherently; something needed be done as early as possible to save the world from any possible catastrophe.

Qazi Irfan
Islamabad, Pakistan
January 10, 2020

Table of Contents

List of Figures

List of Tables

INTRODUCTION

What is the difference in *Murabaha* Financing (*cost plus*) and Lending on Interest (*principal or loan plus*)? This precise query of technical comparison, in modern financial circles, is not raised because of any reason or objection to traditional Islamic contract of *Murabaha* that was permitted and practiced in trading previously but today when the same idea is remodeled to use as an instrument of Islamic financing that bears a semblance to conventional debt financing and lending on interest. Likewise, there is no practical difference in *Murabaha* financing or financing based on other traditional trade contracts defined in Islamic law like *Bai Muajjal* or *Bai Bithaman Ajil* (*deferred payment sale*) therefore the same query may be seen in these contexts too.

The question is logical and so is the criticism and so it be answered logically that shall win through rational and technical arguments of distinction. The innovative people who reshaped the traditional *Murabaha* contract for modern day Islamic financing agreements are so far unsuccessful in producing any convincing judgment of differentiation for alleged similarities. Their inability in doing so seems deep-rooted in the confusion on *Riba* that is not yet resolved within "*who said what analysis*" approach; the author is attempting to answer the query with precise economic and natural reasoning.

Murabaha was a trade contract originally, where the split-up of actual cost of produce and the profit of seller were disclosed to the buyer. The extensive adaptation of this trade contract as a vehicle for Islamic financing is due to this disclosure of price breakup actually, and perhaps the objections and its similarity to '*lending on interest*' are also because of these visible fragments. In spite of the fact that the contemporary Islamic scholars approved this modus operandi as a transitory financing method (*possibly under the law of necessity*) and were not willing to see it as a regular or permanent feature of Islamic financing transactions, yet the fact is – **it is the widely used method** that is not expected to be replaced by other so-called preferred Islamic modes of financing i.e., *Modarabah* and *Musharakah*, in the near future. Experts guesstimate that *Murabaha* financing is almost eighty percent of entire Islamic financing transactions; irrespective of figure's accuracy, everyone accepts that *Murabaha* financing makes the major part of all Islamic financing deals at present.

A less or non-preferential provision is persistently chosen, in practice, over so-called ideal modes that are considered symbolic to Islamic financing. The situation is worth examining putting several questions like **why granting the transitory permission was found necessary; why it failed on the expectations of religious authorities who allowed this for a makeshift or interim use; is there a fault in the permission or in its application** (*the concept* *or the practice where error be if there is any); **is it being misused; do we really have its alternatives to switch over to?*** It is not so simple to answer such questions because the efforts were made with complete sincerity however the results are not as were expected by scholars who invented this? In our social-value parallel, the situation is like a father-son relation, the son is not disobedient too, always seeking father's approval for its actions; now the father shall replace the Fin-Toy given to him earlier if he thinks his son is over playing but who has to play anyway. The desire of father from this infant (*the infancy argument that we usually listen from Islamic Banking and Finance supporters in its justifications and defense*) to drive symbolic heavy financing vehicles (i.e., *Modarabah, Musharakah*) is far from son's reach.

Murabaha financing brand is a new entry to finance industry, somehow challenging the conventional forms of its class on theoretical foundation. We may compare new entrant only within the framework of conventional forms (*i.e., equity, loan and debt financing*) for a genuine distinction. However, the comparison is made without any rethinking to existing conventional forms where a revisit is almost due as well, for instance – if equity is some kind of partnering then what is wrong to consider the **loan form of financing** as another type of 'xyz equity' because financing in itself is not a detached or isolated subject like a loan. The contract of loan (*qard*) is quite different from *protected investment* type of a contract where intention plays a dividing role between the two (*i.e., loan* and *protected investment*); providing a loan, or investing in a business, are two different matters in its essence for the same act of giving money. Intentions cannot be put away from acts. Similar ambiguity exists in Islamic financing thoughts of modern times as well, that restricts the possibility of equity to Profit and Loss Sharing (PLS) method only. Whereas, in practice and reality, there are several situations where PLS may not provide justice, then **why sharing profit and not-sharing loss** (*protected investment*) is not an acceptable mode for economic and justice reasons. The *protected investment* approach is already witnessed in classic *Modarabah*.

Some new beliefs introduced with the emergence of IBF do not find a valid place in previous thoughts e.g., the architects of Islamic Banking and Finance portrays it as an '*assets based*' industry i.e. all forms of financings must involve some assets to make it legal, Islamically. This is a very feeble position that does not cohere with well-known Islamic permissibility order for economic activities. The "*assets based*" drum is beaten so loud and forceful that thinking or voicing against this stance is not listened to. A realistic view on this mistaken belief is also shown in this book to unprejudiced minds.

Financial outlook of Islamic *Murabaha* financing and conventional debt or loan financing is exactly the same; bankers and financial experts do not spot a difference in the two; then what makes them different principally in the eyes of Islamic law i.e., where does the difference lies for the Islamic permissibility of the former and the impermissibility of the other. It's hard for professionals to figure out the difference; tough for legal minds to find in rules. The distinction can only be seen clearly by conceptual or philosophical eye; I have argued that the difference is not financial at all but economic in nature.

Almost all subjects touched here in introduction are dealt with subsequently to some extent. The title is self explanatory of tendency spread throughout the writing; you will find few fresh and innovative ideas as well, like a new classification scheme for *economic activities* is proposed; also presenting an original economic theory; last but not least, attempting to bring thinking towards realism in Islamic financing.

Briefly, in order to answer the query, it is essential to recognize *'what financing is'* prior to investigating the query and working around it; accordingly, starting in a sequence from exploring *'financing'* as generally known so far; followed by *Murabaha* financing model that is in practice; then what exactly is the query; and finally to answer the query in the container of perspectives built in the process; ending with conclusions made.

•••

What is financing?

Financing is the process of providing, acquiring or raising the funds to facilitate or undertake an economic activity (*e.g., production, consumption, trading, education, health, construction, services etc.*) that may not be carried out otherwise or is out of reach without funds.

The term of *financing* is self explanatory, typically used and understood in the context of money, capital or liquid assets. Almost all financing deals are achieved through some motivation or persuasion called upon by (*or on behalf of*) the user of finance, financier, mediator, negotiator etc; all motivations and persuasions can be bracketed together in two broader clusters of purposes i.e., '*For-Profit*' (*commercial*) and '*Not-For-Profit*' (*non-commercial e.g., charitable, religious, communal, falahi[1]*).

The purpose can be served then by way of four basic forms of financing, i.e., *equity*, *loan*, *debt* and *donation*; where donation is specific to non-commercial purpose only, not meant for profit directly (*however donations may potentially or possibly be used indirectly 'for the purpose of profit'*) while the rest three financing forms are applicable to both clusters of purposes.

---

[1] *Urdu term used for 'welfare' meaning*

The financing arrangement of any type brings more than one entities in contact and the relation established out of this interaction needs to be defined in a contract. Obviously, every entity would have its own concerns that it would like to be addressed in the contract. Such concerns usually revolve around the *principal amount, use of funds, profit, loss, risk, liabilities, time, payments, returns, settlement, responsibilities, ownership* etc.

When the basic forms of financing are applied to the vibrant dynamics of purposes, economic activities, the finance providers and the users of funds (e.g., *personal, corporate, public etc.*) at some terms – further branches and types of financings may be characterized.

> *However, essentially the financing en bloc is at least*
> ***A purpose, an economic activity, a form of financing***
> ***applied and a set of terms.***

The holistic view of financing relations starting from this minimal essential, can be elevated such that in a resultant contract, there can be more than one purpose from either cluster (of *for-profit* or *not-for-profit*), any number of economic activities, and more than one forms of financing, whereas terms are usually one plus. The natural and logical possibilities are tremendous.

A sub-class or a brand of financing can be defined as a blend or envelope of at least a basic form (*e.g. equity*) in some specific periphery of situation with a relevant set of terms; for instance *Modarabah* and *Musharakah* are basic *equity forms* of contracts with different sets of terms based on the situation and intentions of involved parties.

Basic forms of financing are four, yet its sub-classes or brands can be numerous that are meant to identify, attribute, standardize or label any blended form of the contract (e.g., bridge financing, commodity *Murabaha*, diminishing *Musharakah* etc.). There is no restriction in inventing a new blend or brand of financing but only by imagination, creativity, and natural progression. The marketers are not behind in using these techniques of identification and financiers have their own marketing brands too.

The financing affairs (*muamlaat*[2]) are predominantly ruled by the laws of the nature and moderately by the guidance or compulsions of the doctrines (*e.g. Islamic codes, Capitalism*) which together forms relevant morals (*ethos*) that are reflected in the terms of the contract.

Briefly, financing leads to achieving a purpose of an intended outcome using some economic course, having endless possibilities. The above is an overall perception of *financing* in my view.

---

[2] *In Islamic Jurisprudence 'Muamlaat' means economic & financial dealings*

Moving further from the common sense of financing to deal with the query, at the first step, we may split the subject of *financing* at its root by laying off half of the purpose cluster to deal only with "*For-Profit*" branch of financing (i.e., commercial).

Financing: For-Profit

Profit is the most dynamic legal form of transferring wealth among the people in an economy; it's the reason of life and the means for living with dignity in a society. Commercial financing has remained an undeniable and natural demand of people and societies. By considering the financing en bloc defined above as basic framework of discussion in this section, we will try to understand each of its building block, its subset elements, related issues and how these factors are treated in competing conventional and Islamic financing.

1. Profit: The Purpose

In this categorical cluster of 'profit', we know that no one works for loss in its sincere and sensible state of mind, *profit is desirable but loss is possible* and a proof to the probability of loss is the manifestation of '*risk*' factor in Islamic and conventional financing contracts. Having said that, we are not discussing '*loss*' and '*risk*' in this section as the two do not fall within the purpose of profit. We will discuss these topics next where they fit exactly in the subsequent sections. Only '*profit*' as a subject is appropriate in this section.

1.1 What is Profit?

The etymological sense of 'profit' shows no change since its origin in history from mid of 13th century; the sustained sense of a common phrase, an expression or a function is the natural strength it illustrates, it is easy to understand its meaning with no or very little efforts. The sense of profit has survived since long that we may describe in several ways, for instance, expressing in our perspective i.e., profit (*faida*[3]) as:

1. A monetary gain desired, expected, or realized from an 'economic activity', or

2. Buying for less and selling for more and making profit, or

3. A positive change in the value of any 'economic input' that incurred as a result of an economic activity and is available in the 'economic output' (exchangeable produce), or

4. Simply an addition to the 'present value' of an exchangeable produce that is or may perhaps be realized in the future, i.e., within 'future value'.

5. An advantage or benefit obtained from a legal form of economic interaction.

---

[3] *Faida is an Arabic term for gain, profit, advantage, benefit etc. and is too old than the origin of profit*

1.2 The Natural Law of Profit?

What you have – is that you have, but what you will gain is not that you had, means the gain or profit has to come from somewhere else. This simple logic implies that a mutual or communal interaction is required for the purpose of profit. An interaction or joint affair is a course of actions or simply a 'process' from getting into contact to exiting from it. The profit may be produced in this process. Since profit has to come from a process, it has three logical states, firstly profit is a desire only, then it's defined at some stage of process, and finally when it is actually realized; unsurprisingly in whole of the process, the quantum of profit in all three states may be the same or can vary from one to the other. The process of profit can be invoked by some motivation or persuasion like a desire alone, but it cannot become a function of the motive; then what constructs it since profit is not a fantasy but a reality.

Profit is a function of time principally, if it were not a function of time then, profit being a motive must had exploded the planet earth by its instant and perpetual behavior. No sentimentality to add emphasize, it is the guess of logic that without its dependency on time, profit will be infinite in zero time i.e. inestimable and immeasurable. Now think of it being tangible and not imaginary, had it not destroyed the earth planet with this perpetual behavior? Logically, a differential of time is essential to assert 'profit', it may be a difference from past time to the present or from present to the future.

If 'profit' were a function of time alone then there remains no reason or motivation for the owner of the finance to do anything by himself or to give his funds to someone else to employ but to sit idle and earn profit by the passage of time. Certainly, nature is not like that as we know, it never happens this way, rationally thus the motive of profit cannot be achieved unless some other function is not included and that other function is the economic activity (a topic in the next section).

Someone may argue – it is only 'economic activity' which constructs profit by rejecting it being dependent of time, then it may also mean that if you call profit by desire only – 'economic activity' shall happen instantly but that seems impossible too. Although the efforts are being made to reduce time element in grasping profit where financial engineers and technologists are at this job day and night in money markets, but still the power remains with GOD (*kun fa ya koon*[4]).

In this natural and realistic perspective, we may define:
'PROFIT' is a function (construct) of time and economic activity.
<u>This is the natural law of profit.</u>

---

[4] *Quran 36:82 – Narrating the power of Allah (SWT) - the Almighty Creator of this universe, when He says "Be!" and it is done.*

The formation of natural law about profit is perfect for its philosophical value, no other generic definition of this quality exists about profit today that we know; neither it lacks in applicability to invite any refutation. It employs the concept of totality encircling all tangible gains that we are aware of today.

In the timeline of every financing deal, logically the differential of time will be from *present to the future* to assert 'profit'. That is – profit from financing is a future concern of all who are looking to make profit from the activity that is being financed. Naturally, the first and the foremost fearful idea that comes in mind as regards to the profit is – will it exist in the future as a result of economic activity or not?

But who knows the future? Profit being the purpose and the focus, every effort and measure will naturally be taken to ensure its maturity and existence in the outcome. It is possible within human intellect to obtain profit in close proximity of estimated target in given conditions. If vital estimations of related activity are worked out sensibly to ensure the purpose of profit in correctness – it is generally acceptable to humans and even doctrines to agree on reasonable variances from estimation since perfect estimation is beyond human ability. The state of desire for the quantum of profit will remain an internal idea until the 'economic output' is put to its potential client for its negotiated worth.

The profit can be defined exactly when the estimated 'future value' of 'economic output' is negotiated with its user, consumer or buyer to set its agreeable 'exchange value'; still the profit may or may not be realized at the time of negotiation. The realization of profit will occur when the transaction is concluded and the interacting entities are technically detached from the relation. The detachment is generally set within the payment terms e.g., on spot or credit or else possible and acceptable to the entities involved.

The stipulation of terms is for the acts by respective performer, if the acts are different, so the terms can be varied too. Therefore in a joint affair – linking of terms to acts or making the terms conditional to some acts is normal, logically. The realization of profit may or may not be linked to, or made conditional to other factors, for instance to the transfer of title or the ownership, or the delivery or else.

In normal circumstances, the profit is realized when the full proceeds of 'exchange value' are received by the owner(s) or the beneficiaries of 'economic output'; at this stage, success can be rated for real profit achieved and its deviation from original expectancy.

Though, the matter of *value* is an unresolved and complex subject like the issue of *Riba*, however in our deliberations here, it is realistic to use *exchange value* concept in place of vague *value*. The exchange value is practical and certain since it's defined by negotiation without the use of any force or indoctrination but by the intent of justice in a mutual affair. Having said that, in the whole process of working for profit, the stage of negotiating the 'exchange value' is extremely important because of two primary reasons:

1. Firstly, the phase of negotiation transforms the *uncertain* state of profit (of desire, expectation) to its *probable, realistic* or *definite* state by fixing an 'exchange value' where all negotiating entities are at their thrust for protecting, maximizing or even enforcing their respective advantages.

2. Secondly, every 'exchange value' has a life that is either defined by some natural factors or set by negotiation; in any case, since 'exchange value' may appreciate or depreciate after expiring its current life hence all factors influencing the life of 'exchange value' shall be exposed during the phase of negotiation.

Negotiation is hence the stage where fairness spirit of profit is built and transcribed in the contract; there are several imperative factors that may influence the kinetics of negotiations. Every influencing factor may have a different meaning for each negotiating entity depending on its status and circumstances. A few of the negotiating aspects (*not all*) are:

1. *The availability of information*: the fair resolve of 'exchange value' is primarily based on the quality of information possessed by all sides that can be different for them individually as negotiators. An *information disparity*, if exist, may result in the exploitation or usurpation of opponents' wealth or rights.

2. *The need and opportunity*: the exchange might be occurring by the cause of need for the one that is seen as an opportunity by the other thus the two causes have entirely divergent motivations, and will obviously put them in different status while negotiating.

3. *Skills and attitudes*: indisputably, the skills and attitudes are always unique to each entity; these personal or professional attributes of negotiating entities play a significant role in the drafting of the contract and the terms and conditions.

4. *Life of 'economic output'*: since every 'exchange value' has a life without exception and one way of setting the life of an 'exchange value' exist during the phase of negotiation. Therefore if this aspect of 'exchange value' is defined in this phase then, principally all life forming or influencing reasons shall be made clear to involved entities, to assert it accurately over the entire period of contract.

5. *Payments of proceeds*: preferably, the payments of proceeds shall be realized within the '*exchange value life*' of economic output otherwise it may be unfair to the beneficiaries.

1.3 Issues in the subject of Profit?

If truth be told, the natural law of profit is violated seriously by the conventional system of interest; what is not profit is also called profit; the arbitrary practices have induced theoretical and practical confusion. What is a legitimate profit is not clear or straightforward in the system of interest? The shadows of conventional system on emerging Islamic banking and finance (IBF) thinking, are distorting the Islamic concept of profit as well. Although, each issue in itself is a separate subject of discussion; however these are just highlighted here very briefly to move on with the core subject.

Which definition to apply

Though, the analogous words used interchangeably to designate *profit* like *gain, benefit, advantage* etc., are equally understood for the sense of *profit*, yet a notable confusion exist in the projected meaning of *profit* given by subject specialism practices. For instance bankers, economists, and accounting people will define *profit* from their own perspectives of subjects using their own yardsticks for measuring and estimation of *profit*, e.g., wealth, types of banking interests etc. The issue is what definition to apply in a picky case when according to the standards of 'accounting', a profit is realized but as said by the standards of economics the wealth is rather decreased, or not changed, so one profited or not?

Fixed and Variable Profit

This is though not an issue in conventional system; but it's a notable issue in current Islamic thinking. The source of these issues is probably the poor principles derived from traditional Islamic contracts and also the subject of *Riba*. In reality the taking and averting risk, sharing propensity are all different shades of human instinct (*fitrah*); the nature does not deny the desire of fixed or variable *profits* either. In principle by nature, if the economic activity produces a real and evident *profit* (i.e., **the existence of profit is confirmed**) then it does not matter if the sharing or distribution of *profit* among its beneficiaries is agreed on a fixed, variable or a mix of fixed and variable method. This is a realistic stance on *profit* and a logical position but not accepted rather is a reason of conflict in many circumstances of profit.

Bench-marking Issue

Interest based conventional banking instruments are bench-marked to LIBOR or KIBOR type inter-bank interest-rate standards. In the transformation process of conventional banking to Islamic banking – it was easy to convert the terminology of banking-interest to "*mark-up*" or "*profit*" but the making or developing of its own bench-mark was not an easy task; owing to this lacking, Islamic banks opted to use bench marks that were already existing in conventional banking system to standardize their newly developed or converted Islamic banking instruments. This practice of linking the mark-up or profit with a variable standard which is established upon the prohibited function of Interest, is never accepted by a large faction of Islamic scholars even by those who allowed this for a temporary use. Certainly, there are serious repute problems for Islamic finance in using interest-bench-marks but the most serious issue is when this conventional reference varies during the period of Islamic financing contract and effects the expectation and realization of profit, thus inducing the uncertainty. The feature of uncertainty in Islamic contracts is a sensitive issue (e.g., *gharar*[5]). Is there a way to evaluate the uncertainty created by the use of conventional bench-marks? This is an issue, not dealt with to delineate risk and gharar; and its Islamic permissibility is not even established in the first place.

Penalty Issue of Profit

For the repayment of funds in a financing contract, fixed or periodic payment liabilities are created on due dates. If the due payment liability is not discharged on time then imposing penalties is a common practice in conventional system; unfortunately, almost the same practice is adopted in Islamic finance operations using

---

[5] *Gharar is a level of uncertainty rationally unacceptable, whereas risk is rationally acceptable.*

a feeble pretext of giving the penalty amount to charity; though such penalties can affect the defined *profit* but the issue is the practice, very questionable from Islamic point of view – *can you impose penalty in the first place? What is its Islamic legal justification from Shariah since the concept of the holy Quran on the matter of being late in discharging liability is significantly different and quite humane, that is ignored*; such practices are damaging the philosophy of Islam in fact.

1.4 How Profit is treated

The equitable distribution of wealth in any society is directly related to the fair mechanism of profit and just wages prevailing in the social order. In power corridors of class societies – the instrument of profit is one of the most influential tools used for social manipulation; the functional economic philosophy of society that defines and streamlines the mechanism of profit is ultimately decisive in establishing distributive justice. The fact is, there is no society existing in the world as of today that is said to be following the Islamic economic doctrine of profit; there is none though the philosophy exists. In our case of financing 'for profit' here, the comparison of treating the profit is based on recent conventional and Islamic banking practices. The practical handling of the subject of *profit* in two doctrines is poles apart in reality though the apparent outlook is not so divergent, let us see as how *profit* is practically treated in the two doctrines, with little commentary of mine a few places.

In Conventional Finance

I know and you know that who knows better than conventional money lenders, financiers and bankers that money (*finances*) needs to be engaged in some way to earn *profit*? Simply they recognize the must function of economic activity for the purpose of profit but this recognition and its reality is not reflected in contracts where they make *profit*, a function of time alone. By ousting the economic activity and its relevant matters in a money lending contract – the **natural law of profit** is confronted and contradicted at the root. No alternate law or stance is given by conventional lenders to justify the so-called *profit*, the wrong is integrated in contract at its inception; no other terms or clause, whatsoever, stipulated in the contract can repair this contractual fault.

Will this 'contractual fault' do some harm to anyone in or out of the loop or not and if it does then to whom? No such 'contractual fault' is admitted by them because it is legally supported by law, but the law is without any reason supporting it so the law in itself is illegal. There must be some natural or economic law of *profit* that shall justify their practice. There is no foundational or natural law ever proposed for the construct of *profit* in their doctrine, conventional advocates do not have any convincing answer that can favour their position. The harm from conventional practices is though evident, e.g., forced inflation that affects everyone badly.

Albeit, the point is very clear that *profit* is neither a function of time alone nor it can be achieved without 'economic activity', i.e., the finance provider and user of finance are essential for each other to materialize their intended *profits*, then what puts them at disparity to expel the concerns of one side all together? It is less important that who exerts the force of expulsion, more important is that exclusion of activity concerns occurs in the contract. It could be muscles disparity in favour of finance provider, or information disparity to user side or pressing need against one or anything else in any one's favour who is taking undue advantage of that in making *profit*.

It may be argued that it goes in the benefit of the two and they mutually agree to expel 'economic activity' concerns together, but that is not an acceptable stance by any stretch of imagination and one may ask:

1. *Why?* Is it not the need of both to engage in 'economic activity'?

2. *How?* Can you jump to the target of *profit* over the process?

3. *If,* they don't care for the economic activity which has to produce what they intend to achieve, then how they will do justice with it?

4. *Or,* if there is nothing in the activity that shall be taken care of, will it mean that there is no 'loss' or 'risk' concerns as well, but they are serious about 'risk', where in activity or in the heavens?

5. *If,* they intend to do justice with economic activity for their own purpose of assuring *profit* then how they can expel the concerns of the activity even mutually?

These are conceivable queries bringing morality of 'lending on interest' practice in question that seems as not being respected. What they earn this way can't be regarded as legitimate *profit* but something else since *profit is profit only when it comes through the natural law of profit*, authenticity of all acts comes only from some divine, natural or human laws; legitimacy cannot be upheld without respecting and obeying the rules of law; natural law of *profit* is the universal rule in nature and cannot be circumvented in any circumstances if to earn *profit* legally. The evasion of natural law here will imply that we can alter rules and claim legitimacy. How someone can fetch the authority to alter principles from within a financing transaction? If one can do then everyone gets the right even looters, plunderer, thieves and bribe-takers to justify what they plunder. There is no doctrine of *profit* in conventional lending system.

In Islamic Finance

On the contrary, in Islamic doctrine, the natural law of profit is not only accepted and upheld but a logical and systematic purification process of profit is devised for further refined legitimacy. As we expect from every religion to think good about men and society, the same goes true with Islam but with perfection where no part of life and discipline is left unaddressed. The subject of economic interactions is rather elevated, proclaiming the precise set of guidelines; according to these tenets, a profit may be justified by the natural law of profit but still it may not be good to the people and society thus not approved in Islam. The Islamic sanitizing structure of profit is primarily organized in two logical blocks i.e., *selection* and *execution*, each having two stages therein. In a top-down order as below:

1. Selection

a) Economic Activities: Human intent is the place where results are planted; acts are seen by the intent it had and so is the outcome from the act or the activity. Naturally, intents cannot be forbidden but the act or activity can be; when an act or activity is prohibited, it simply implies that the intent is blocked and thus the unwarranted results. This simple philosophy is devised for the selection of activities or barring of unwarranted activities in Islam; the segregation is made at the root in the 'concept of *profit*' and the process of legitimating *profit* starts when selecting an 'economic activity', for instance when trade is allowed – it means you can earn profit through trading; when gambling is prohibited or when hoarding is outlawed, says any gain from such activities is not a legal gain in the eyes of Islamic law; though the list of prohibited activities is very small but strictly any gain from prohibited activities is not a legal profit in Islamic value system. One can only earn an islamically legitimate *'profit'* from 'economic activities' that are permitted in Islamic doctrine.

b) Subject or Substance: It is not only the acts or activities which can be harmful for the men or society but there are stuffs that are also hurtful and unhealthy for the people and communities. Therefore a second tier of prohibition in the legitimacy of *profit* is set by segregating the subjects and materials. The reason to outlaw the prohibited stuff is usually contained within the substance itself; for instance alcohol is prohibited for the reason of its intoxication impact; narcotics is banned for the reasons in itself; no 'economic activity' in Islamic doctrine is allowed for the manufacturing, trading, or consumption of these forbidden products; means alcohol and narcotics are prohibited substances in permitted activities.

2. Execution

a) Principles: Indeed, the list of excluded activities, substances or stuffs is very small, all the rest is allowed. However, the filtered selections are then put through a set of principles in the execution phase. This can well be explained by the case in hand. The act of lending is a permitted activity; the money as a substance is also on approved list; so the selection is okay in both respects, confirming that lending the money is a permissible act in Islamic value system. You are allowed to undertake a lending the money transaction but execution is guided by few principles set in Islamic doctrine. For instance, it is not allowed to put the condition of returning more than what is lent i.e., charging excess or *Riba* is not allowed in the activity that was otherwise permitted in the first place; in another instance, it is not allowed to undertake any activity having rationally unacceptable risk or uncertainty called *Gharar*. The selection phase is relatively clear matter perhaps because of the nature of directives for personal or individual's compliance, but the execution in the hierarchy of *profit* sanitization, is somewhat convoluted owing to conceptual reasons and unclear definitions; this stage is a real test of practicing Islamic tenets with spirit where utmost care is insisted to draft the terms of executing the activity so.

b) Performance: It is not only emphasized to draft the terms of execution with the spirit of directed beliefs but to fulfill them in letter and spirit too, i.e., must do exactly as agreed, discharge your liabilities exactly as implied, must fulfill promises exactly as committed, in order to satisfy the one who is expecting all this from you. Even very small tips are advised and demanded by the believers while performing the activity, for instance about the conduct (*e.g.* weigh accurately, be helpful, honour your commitments), and prohibiting conducts (*e.g.* cheating, lying, dishonesty) from start to finish.

This is very simple engaging strategy in the process of profit, that is to say - if a list of forbidden activities, subjects and substances is prepared, then all other activities, subjects and substances are permissible and available for Islamic financing (**the prohibition list is very small indeed**). If existing conceptual confusions are removed for the execution phase (primarily *Riba*), then there we have legitimate profit from Islamic point of view. Though, the profit legalizing code is simple, yet in present state of inaccurate selection list and forced confusion induced from the miscalculations of modern scholars for their analysis of traditional contracts, who knows better than those seeking Islamically legitimate profit that how difficult is it today.

1.5 Conceptual dilemmas in Islamic Finance

The noble *Fiqh*[6] scholars of *Islam* had left behind an incomparable heritage of useful principles, standards, contracts, terms and conditions for economic dealings. It's noticeable all of their efforts were focused on single prime objective to establish justice in these contracts. They handled situations as existed at that time but not all that as we find today. In this legacy, the *profit* is not

---

[6] Islamic Jurisprudence

detached from economic activity anywhere; the time is given its due role to assert the *profit*. They formulated standard contracts for given circumstances with exact applicable set of terms for the situations in question; these contracts are now part of Islamic *Fiqh* serving as a reference to make advancements in this era.

The world has changed significantly from the time when the grand *Fiqh* was developed initially; business needs, techniques and practices have gone through an evolution process of development, new disciplines have emerged like the fields of economics, banking etc. The occurrence of this transformation can be judged easily by acknowledging new economic activities that were not present then e.g., the creation and development of intellectual properties (e.g. *software*), the involvement of third-parties in activities (*i.e., banks and financing institutions including Islamic*) etc.

Financing by intermediaries is a new phenomenon of recent age that was not present in golden Islamic era of *Fiqh*; obviously therefore, we don't find third party related concerns in contracts developed by earlier *Fiqh* architects. Naturally and logically thus, some value is required to be added to the intellectual base of their work to cohere with current demands; such efforts are rather binding because of one primary reason at least that with the involvement of financing mediators in 'economic activities', highly sensitive issues including that of *Riba* (*with its unresolved status*) are prompted and forcing other values to change which originally had no dispute in their perception and understanding, for instance, the wisdom and logic of model contracts (e.g. *Modarabah*) is distorted; the sense of *profit* is confined and entirely connected to assets only. In our existing circumstances, we must accept the fact that our current scholars have not been successful in demonstrating the ability to insert exact sense of 'economic interaction' in newly developed contracts to establish justice as our predecessors were able to do in their circumstances.

It is somehow misread by our contemporary Islamic minds in finance that legality of a money transaction comes from 'assets', or the *profit* exists in 'assets' alone. This is really poor thinking on their part; there is no sense in locking the financing transactions with assets, it can create a deadlock situation in a system of money to function efficiently. One such stalemate situation is witnessed in the Federal Shariat Court[7] where the state bank of Pakistan, SBP, has built several of its points in defense against *Riba* verdict stating that there are not enough assets to convert to *Shariah* compliant modes required for bank's operations as per Islamic beliefs. Though the position taken by SBP is mala fide, but the argument is based on the very stance of 'assets backed' hypothesis presented by current IBF advocates. Sooner

---

[7] *Shariat Petition No.30/L OF 1991 - M/S Farooq Brothers etc. Vs United Bank Ltd etc.*

or later, these feeding minds of Islamic banking and finance have to retreat from this feeble and hard-line position on 'assets backed' hypothesis. The posturing and labeling of Islamic Banking and Finance industry as an 'assets backed' industry is a self deception stance that will keep this industry forever under the control of conventional money system. This is definitely a fallacy about money business, economic activities and profit primarily because of two conceptual reasons:

Firstly, the legitimacy of profit, before any doctrinal assessment or cleansing, has to come from the natural law of profit that is a function of economic activity and that can happen with no assets involved. The process of Islamic permissibility of profit is a post hoc permission of naturally legal profit. In this process, the selection of economic activities is already done at the root where the reason of rejecting an activity is within the activity. Then subjects and stuffs are barred for the reasons in it. The blanket use of assets to accept economic activity for financing is incoherent with Islamic process; assets have no quality to decide on 'economic activity', neither it can become a 'function of profit' in anyway then from where this *quasi-Islamic* concept of 'assets backed' is inducted, perhaps from prevalent confusion about *Riba* and differentiating it from trade. The assets can merely be an object in a process of economic activity where it can serves as a carrier of 'exchange values' or as means for the transference of profits only.

Secondly, making the existence of assets as a basic qualifying criteria to financing prospects will also imply that the first cannon of segregating economic activities is also assigned to assets i.e., all economic activities will not qualify for Islamic finance if not involving assets. As said above, assets hold no such rationale to classify economic activities for its Islamic permissibility or elimination that has already been done at the root, and neither such responsibility was ever given to assets in the religion previously; therefore modern advocates of Islamic finance shall provide an underlying principle for this segregation. Here it may be remembered that economic activities are impermissible in Islam for the reasons *ab intra*. If the 'assets backed' claim has any reason in *Riba* then that shall be addressed at the level of executing the activity and not at the level of selecting the economic activity.

It is worthy to reiterate this sensitive permissibility dilemma; Islam prohibits an activity or the object for a reason of it from within itself (*ab intra*); all activities and all objects are permissible that are not forbidden explicitly. The prohibition always has some reason of it, there is no reason ever told by current scholars for not allowing 'no assets' based activities, explicit or implied. If anything new is to be outlawed in modern times and to be expelled from the ambit of qualifying for Islamic financing, that must have some reason of it *ab intra*, no matter whether an assets is involved or not. The fallacy of "assets backed industry" has indeed expelled a major and workable part of 'economic activities' from Islamic financing options. In basic economic sense, an already reduced and filtered set of chances is further slashed without any basis in the original code of Islamic belief.

In addition to this naïve dilemma of assets, another philosophical lapse is committed by modern scholars for reversing the order of intellect in the hierarchy of intellects (*there are at least four basic levels of intellect, the top level domain of intellect is 'the reason of law', next is 'the legal domain', followed by executive & administrative domains*). The law and rules of law are made for a belief to uphold or enforce the belief in practice (implying the belief has the reason of law or the principle); unluckily, our ingenious modern Islamic scholars have deduced the reasons and principles from the rules of law and enforcing to believe on; this lapse has literally confined the entire spectrum of 'economic interactions' within the realm of contracts established in earlier *Fiqh* e.g., *Modarabah, Musharakah, Murabaha etc.*

For instance, in orthodox *Modarabah* contract, there is a condition that if loss is incurred in venture – then the finance provider (*Rub-ul-maal*) will bear it; from this situational condition, our modern scholars have deduced the principle that ***loss shall always be borne by the finance provider***. This deduction in many cases may result to injustice, tarnishing the philosophy of Islamic doctrine. The small individual depositors and investors to Islamic banks and financing institutions are treated as *Rub-ul-maal* (capital providers), Islamic banks and IFIs as agent, are free to provide this money to very wealthy business groups on *Modarabah* basis, even to those who have enough liquidity of their own and can do the same activity with their own finance. If any loss is accrued in *Modarabah* activity financed by IBF then by virtue of the said derived principle, the loss shall be assigned to these small capital providers where many of them may not be able to bear this loss. No justice is seen in this state of affairs, no logical man can agree to such assignment of loss in given situation. The reason of this condition in traditional *Modarabah* was – since *Mudarib* do not have the capacity to bear the loss and has done his part per contract, naturally then the loss shall be borne by the capital provider, accordingly this clause was put in the contract. The only principle, if to deduce from this contract should have been that the **loss shall be borne by the one who can bear the loss** to cohere with the humane philosophy of Islam.

Such inelegant deductions on fragile premises are irritable oversight and failures of current scholarship that has reduced the whole nature of the most civilized code of Islamic economic interactions within so short latitude of old contracts; thus it's impossible (*naturally*) and illogical (*in belief*) to accept this reduction which destroys the concept of *profit* as well.

2. Economic Activity

The modern economic thoughts of western world are though dominant but acutely lacking philosophical coherence and accurate definitions in some very basic subjects. For instance, if it's asked 'what is an economic activity', then instead of getting a reasonable definition, we get an answer in category list of economic activities i.e., production, distribution and consumption, some also include exchange as fourth category. You get a list of economic activities but no answer as what actually an 'economic activity' is? What is common or essential function in these classes that is viewed as an economic activity is not made clear? Knowing the commonality is so considered necessary because, for instance, as of the production activity – economic output from the activity is available with some addition or modification to the economic input or without any destruction; whereas on the other hand, from a consumption class of economic activity – the input to economic process may totally be consumed leaving nothing as output in a tangible form, the two results are contradictory then what is common in both to be regarded as economic activity?

Honestly, these categories in conventional thinking do not even cover all natural possibilities of economic activities; inevitably we need to perceive an answer to the query of 'economic activity' definition that shall exhibit a universal and suitable sense inclusive of all economic incidents in nature. Instead of looking from a narrow angle of what is measureable and accountable, i.e. as opposed to the present restricted conception of accredited production, consumption and distribution of tangible or intangible goods and services, we shall include all those factors, intents and occurrences that are economic in nature but not recognized in current economic thinking. For instance, it is mere fallacy that man's motivation to work is its needs and the intent of benefit only (*that is a reduction of men's nature*), while men also work for pride, honour, praise, spirituality etc.; then we know nature creates and amends value of its products without any intervention from man i.e., without involving his labour or intellect or machines even; these are definitely incidents of economic nature, measurable and accountable as well if we need to see from current methodology, yet such happenings do not find a valid place in traditional economic philosophies.

In such conceptually lacking perspective, obviously we may desire, a concept shall be existing able enough to enfold all conceivable economic activities, valid from the inception of human's interactions to this age and time. After much efforts to locate one such idea either in descriptive or pictorial form, when no success was seized unluckily, I urged myself to try developing a model concept to define 'economic activity' that may be suitable for above cited perimeter, yet it does not mean that someone had not done it before, may be or may not be, simply I have no evidence.

2.1 The missing reasons of coherence

Intelligent minds having economic intellect are not satisfied with the vague answer on economic activity, it seems outdated to them as well, primarily because the progression made in this social discipline of economics is left out. For instance, new dimensions of economic activities have emerged where the noteworthy human intellect is the sole partaker in the creation of value but these novel activities do not fit anywhere in present classes of economic activities. Historically, as we know, *in pre- and post-industrialized economic philosophies, human contribution as input to an economic activity is always beholden as a provider of labour,* i.e., *the acts of human are based on his energy stores as a rule while the function of his intellect was limited to directing his energy stock to perform those acts.* While in present information age, an additional blend of man's innate features has emerged to a significant extent, i.e., *human intellect is the actual input to an economic activity and his energy stock has limited contribution that is - just to sustain his ability in providing the intellect.*

This is more than evident now that the contribution of human intellect as a key economic input in creating an economic product of utility is well recognized in this era, for instance, creation of intellectual properties like patents, software, media and various communication products; recently a new phenomenon of virtual world is turned up after the spread of Internet that offers virtual products to trade using virtual money that is convertible to legal money. Such significant activities cannot be neglected for having an economic character. Though, intellect was not silent previously as well but it was never familiar as a regular primary contributor to economic activities.

2.2 Defining Economic Activity

For the most precise definition of 'economic activity' to satisfy the intelligent economic intellect of modern times, the model concept presented here is comprising basic building-blocks relevant to any possible economic activity of all times. The comprehensive schematic also includes a valid place for nature's role (*although that is ever-present but not represented in traditional theories*); secondly the 'human nature' for its inclusive economic character; and thirdly, contribution of human intellect as a notable form of input to an 'economic activity'.

In below illustration, few building-blocks are placed according to their logical positions and relevance in an activity. The primary or fundamental building-blocks are just three i.e., economic input, economic process and economic output. A brief description of primary as well as few associated components is given followed by an appropriate new definition suggested for 'economic activity'. Logically, an innovative classification scheme of economic activities is devised next based on concept model of economic activity.

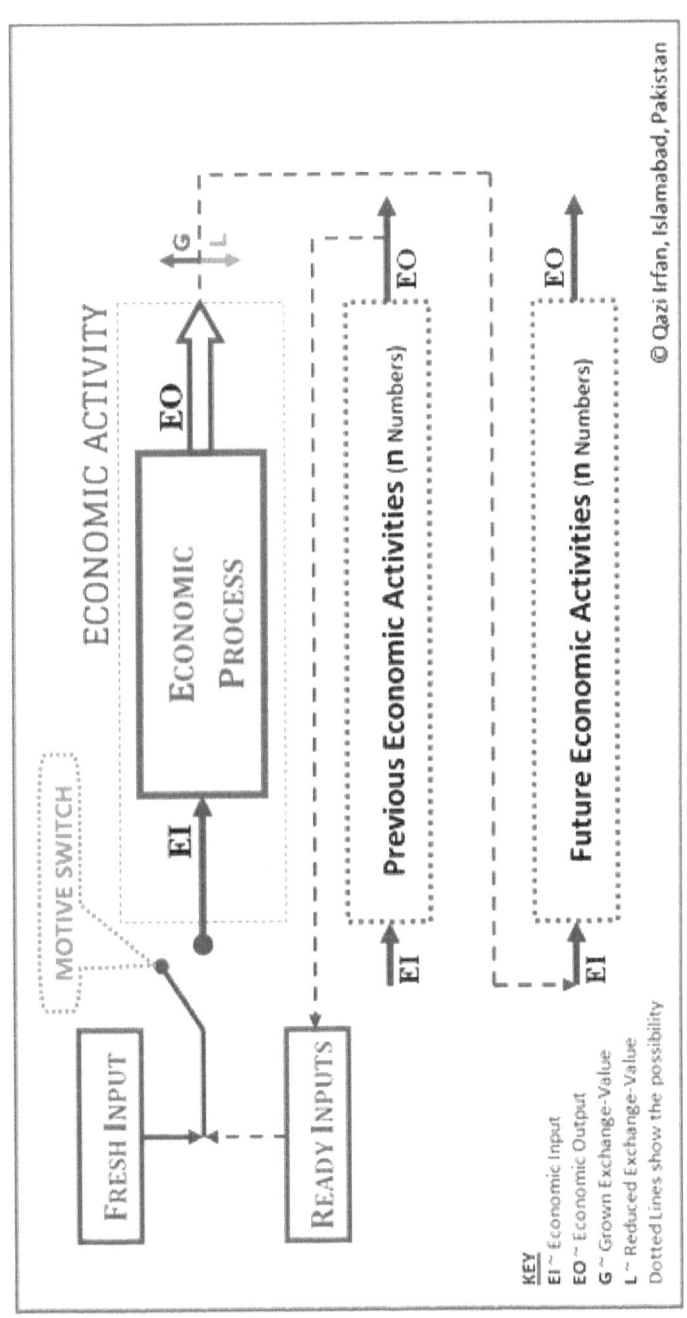

Figure 1 : Economic Activity

53

Fresh Input

The concept of *fresh input* is original - that the input has never gone through an economic process before. In quick minds certainly, a question may arise why we are creating such classes in economic inputs? In fact there are valid economic reasons in doing so, primarily for its meaningful fresh exchange-value economic quality, the *fresh input* traits will be exhibited in another set-task that I intend to undertake afterward. Though now, this provision may help in measuring and estimation of the gross domestic use of natural and human resources.

Fresh input is either supplied by the nature or exists within humans' innate capacity or created by order e.g., unclaimed land having no owner previously; renewable energies, rain etc., then human intellect is one and his energy is another form (*not labour unless transformed into acts impelled by motives*), and we might take newly created money (*fiat*) that was never put to work before as another example of fresh input etc. etc. The entire traits of *Fresh Inputs* can be rationalized as the nature (*unclaimed land and resources, processes, divine acts etc.*), human intellect, human energy, and capital by order.

Ready Input

Ready input is an *economic output* from a previously concluded economic activity; supplied as input to this economic process. Rationally, all previous economic outputs are properties of some owner(s) or will have some claims of ownership, and if have no owner then we might consider these as waste or redundant. Entire identification of *Ready Inputs* can be rationalized as the properties in ownership or having claims of ownership like (*land, materials, machines, tools, capital, skills etc.*). *Ready Inputs* are plenteous, therefore further specialty or classes of properties may be organized based on its purposeful quality or function; e.g., some properties are productive in nature i.e., helpful in other economic processes; another property class having the quality to serve as a carrier of exchange-value; few can serve as a catalyst of changing value etc. *Ready inputs* have a very wide spectrum in fact having the possibility to establish sub-traits class schemes based on several attributes specifically on logical and practical facts.

Motive Switch

What we do or intend to do, have or must have some motive(s), that aims are actually the formative causes of life and work without doubt. In a broad sense, all '*for profit*' and '*not for profit*' causes of actions that push us to involve in an economic process include but not limited to our needs, competition, opportunity, pride, praise, spirituality, honour, help, benefit, greed or any instinct of kind within individuals or purpose of non-living entities that are meaningful for them to survive, sustain or thrive; and to satisfy or gratitude or seeking pleasure or whatever man intend to achieve, and do at will or compulsion. This is to say all inclusive 'human nature' and 'business purposes'. *It is possible that all inputs are available and ready to put in a process at hand but the reality of motive is such that if no motive is available then no economic activity may ever take place.*

Economic Input (EI)

Simply, *economic input* is the sum of all ingredients, tangible or intangible that are required as input for the intended 'economic process'; may include a mix of both *'fresh input'* and *'ready input'* or just one of the two, as required for the economic process to function; when the motive is applied, all inputs will become functional *economic inputs.*

Economic Process (EP)

The nucleus of every economic activity is the process made up of a sequence of events or course of actions to produce natural or intentional outcome. An *economic process is any act, work, function, or process to happen for creating, adding, modifying or transferring the* **no worth or substantial worth to some other form of substantial worth, tangible or intangible, having an exchange-value or impact-value as the result.** The most important thing about *'economic process'* is that besides working with materials, energies and intellect, it also shapes or creates *value perception* of economic outputs to make it such that it shall be acceptable to others and this is an extraordinarily fascinating thing for society. It means **all efforts and intelligence put in an economic process** to produce something of value, suitable and acceptable to the people of society **ultimately translates in to the fact of knowing the people more and more, this 'to and fro' perfection experience in economic process and people's**

56

acceptability is the phenomenon of societal evolution. Knowing people is good to serve them however other side of the fact of knowing the people by experience is open for negative commercialism since knowing their weaknesses may result in their exploitation too.

Economic Output (EO)

This is what every sponsor of economic activity must be looking or working for, because what they intend to achieve is held by or served by the *'economic output'*. In effect, *economic output* in itself may not be so significant but the purpose and results expected from it are always important. The complete effect of *economic output* may be more than the original purpose or expectation i.e., some extra is also achieved than estimated. Principally thus, an all-inclusive economic traits of *economic output* shall be recognized by the economic intellect of today. In usual economic theories generally though, *there is a deadlock in theoretical flow of economic subjects soon after the role of money is ended.* In brief, likewise the process, *economic output* might also have other implications, social or else, even if the activity was undertaken only to make some profit from it.

In fact, the canvas of *'economic process'* and *'economic output'* may also be seen independent of the purposes i.e., irrespective of *'for profit'* or *'not for profit'* reasons, to analyze economic outcome alone. We shall expect that an *economic output* may have good and bad results concurrently for the people and the society. In normal economic course though, most studies are conducted for results expected or planned from it but rarely for the unforeseen effects. One may ask why is it important to study that was not planned. The answer is simple, because it affects the people and society. It may not be graceless to reiterate here for the reason of it be very important, that a comprehensive economic character of *economic output* shall be measured and analyzed for its purposeful and derivative results together; it will be the real economics and true branch of social science if so complied; otherwise perfection in economic thinking may be compromised.

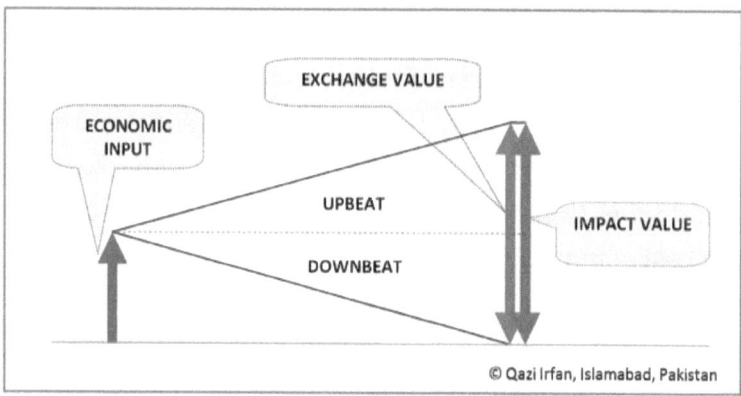

Figure 2 : Economic Output

Though an economic activity *'for profit'* is meant to get some profit from it, however as referred above, we may expect other outcome as well i.e., besides serving the motive of profit to the sponsors, it produces some impact as well to the people involved in the activity or not, and the impact planned from the activity or not.

The hybrid purposes and hybrid results, by intent, are possible from economic activities and its outcome but such are complex types to introduce or discuss here. In minimal approach segregating though, we may create a basic academic division of *'economic output'* for the two realms of motives i.e., resulting from *'for profit'* and *'not for profit'* purposes, designated by *'exchange value'* and *'impact value'* respectively as shown in Figure 2 above.

An analysis or judgment on the results of *'economic output'* must be seen in relation to the *'economic input'* and the *'motive of activity'* together, for the reason that these two will define the state of circumstances prior to the activity. It will be helpful in realistic conclusions and to measure true rate of success. For instance, if we need to estimate results obtained from a *'not for profit'* activity to reduce poverty, it may be evaluated in view of poverty indicators now available after the impact of the activity and the differential of indicators in relation to the input and motive together.

2.3 New definition suggested

I feel no hesitation in reiterating that the *'value'* is a complex and unresolved subject like the issue of *Riba*; there is no indisputable definition of *value*, confusion and vagueness persist about *value*, it is nonfigurative, non-measurable thing for its individualistic meanings in the field of economics. Yet, the mutualistic idea of *'exchange-value'* has specific meanings as it is figurative and measurable by known applied practices; similarly for almost the same reasons, it's simple to comprehend the meaning of '*impact value*' as well. Thus in brief, the *exchange-value* and *impact-value* are clear and resolved expressions though both are derived from unresolved '*value*' in the first place. What changes in an *economic process* is the '*value*' in real or abstract terms. The value put in as '*economic input*' to the activity, going through a change and came out as an '*economic output*' is valued practically by any negotiation or assessment methods to define *exchange value* or *impact value* respectively.

Since we have a universal function in all economic activities hence we may define **economic activity** as:

> **Economic Activity is a function of creating or amending the value of exchangeable or transferable goods and services.**

Thus by definition – it is must that a change of value (real or abstract) shall occur by the activity to qualify it as an economic activity; a real change of value is the differential of input and output exchange-values while an abstract change of value is the differential of worth realized by the recipients of economic output.

The *exchange-value* and *impact-value* are the certain states of uncertain *value*; more accurately or in other words, *exchange-value* is the certain state of uncertain *value* and *impact-value* is the approximate or assessed state of uncertain *value* (e.g. comfort, calories etc.)

In query subject of *for-profit* financing activity which is about *exchange-values* only, the change or differential of values as a result of economic activity is measured by the difference of *exchange-values* at the input and the output of economic process.

Virtually, the net value of an *economic input*, in terms of its *exchange-value*, can be zero, for instance the solar photovoltaic input to solar power plant; similarly the *exchange-value* of an *economic output* can be zero too, for instance when electrical energy is consumed fully in work done by it. Logically, the function of changing the value can vary *from zero exchange value* to some *definite exchange value* having a life and *to zero exchange-value* again, that is to say –from the creation of value to its total destruction and anything in between. The *change of value* can be recognized either in the *economic output* itself or by the recipient(s) of the *economic output*.

2.4 New classification scheme proposed

The process to change the value may have only four rational possibilities i.e., by creation, augmentation, transference, and diminution. Let us first see the chart of new classification as below and then each category is explained a bit:

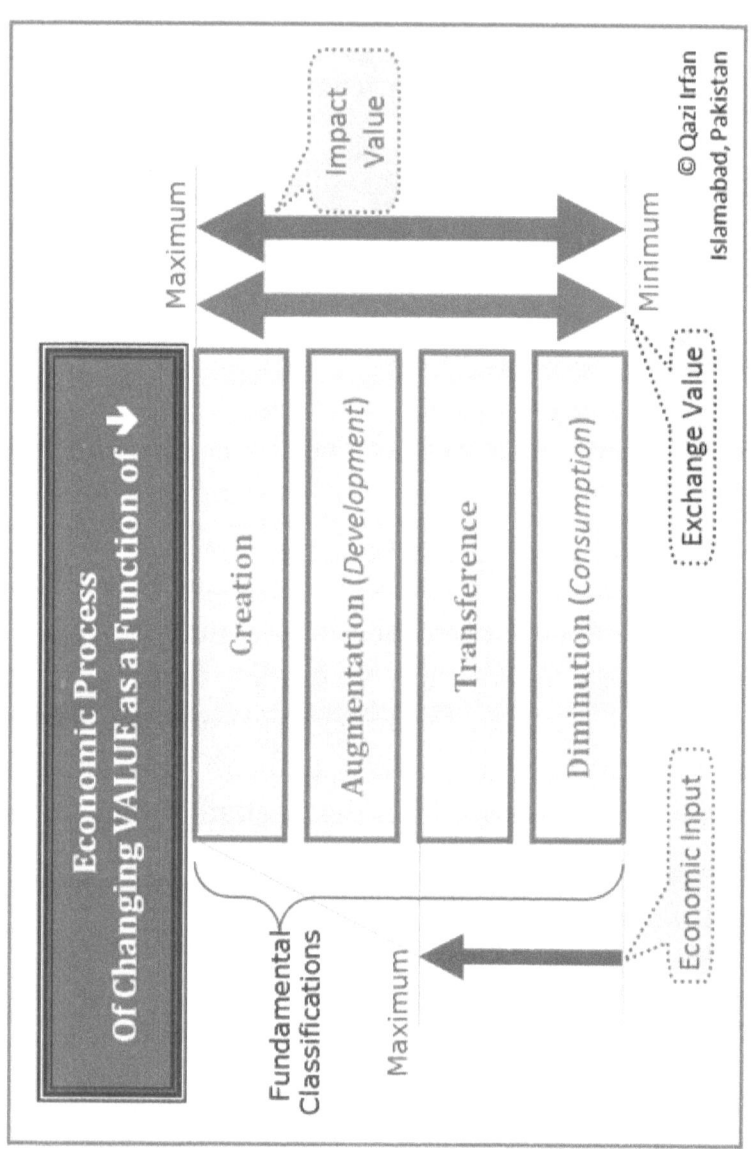

Figure 3 : New Classification Scheme proposed

Creation

Where the *economic input* entering the process has zero *exchange value*, the creation activity inducts some worth through *economic process* resulting in setting the *exchange value* of *economic output* greater than zero. For instance, a process to convert the sun light (*free fuel, a fresh and free of cost economic input having zero exchange value before undergoing the process*) into electrical power having an *exchange value* for each unit produced. This photovoltaic conversion of sun light (solar energy) into electrical power is a perfect creation type of economic activity. We may remind that the setting up the process i.e., installing the solar plant was a previous activity of establishing the process.

Augmentation

Where *economic input* has some *exchange value* at the time of entering the *economic process*, the augmentation activity will further add some worth to it through the *economic process* resulting in setting the *exchange value* of resultant *economic output* greater than the *exchange value* that was put in i.e., the *economic input*. Such are the most common type of economic activities primarily dominated by production and development operations.

Transference

This is unique *economic activity* where the change of value does not occur in *economic input* as such but *by the activity for the recipient* of *economic output*, notably -

the transference activity will transfer the same worth through *economic process* to its beneficiary or receiver for whom the *change of wdvalue* occurred.

Diminution or Consumption

Where *economic input* has some *exchange value* at the time of entering the *economic process*, the diminution (*reduction or consumption*) activity will reduce its worth through *economic process* resulting in the *exchange value* of *economic output* less than the *exchange value* of the *economic input* that was fed in; the reduction or erosion may even result in zero *exchange value* at the output.

In view of this new classification sense, following is a shortened list of examples in each group of economic activity to understand the spirit of tagging:

Table 1 : Examples under New Classification

Economic Process and Examples
Creation
Nature's Creation of Resources and Products Conversion of renewable energies Intellectual Creations by Humans Inventions

Augmentation (*Development*)

Discovery/Extraction of Natural Resources
Research & Developments
Infrastructure Developments
Human Resource Developments
Agricultural and Industrial Productions
Natural growth of value in natural Products
Trading of real advantages

Transference

Inheritance
Distribution
Services
Trading of perceptive advantages
Gambling

Diminution (*Reduction*)

Consumptions by humans and machines
Natural reduction of value in natural Products
Trading by Discounting or Liquidation

2.5 Examples of new classification scheme

Few examples may help to comprehend the unique way of thinking offered in fresh definition of economic activity and subsequent classification. One may notice the common reason and perfect coherence within the definition and its classes. Regrettably, such a precision and coherence is missing in current economic thoughts on the subject of economic activity where neither any rationality nor any reason of connectivity is found, only categories that are even incompatible in meanings to assert a subjective relevance between them. Given that the *economic activity* is the function of changing value, some distinctive examples are as below:

Example 1

A farmer harvested a crop of basmati rice (*economic output*) by employing an agriculture production process and using some *economic inputs* (including his labour). His product of rice certainly has an *exchange value* and he sells his stock. The buyer of basmati rice knowing that if he keeps it for some time, the aroma and taste of rice will improve and therefore its value (*i.e., exchange value if he sells it further or the impact value to satisfy his demand of taste if he consumes it*). In our thinking about economic activity, a change of value has taken place in effect by keeping the rice for some time; this increase in value (*change of value*) is attributable to nature only since no other work or process was applied by any man or machine or else during this period when the change of value was happening.

This is the recognition of nature's role in amending the value of its produce resulting in profit for the owner of rice. The input was rice; economic activity is done by nature since it increased the value of rice at the output, producing profit exactly as per the natural law of profit. Yet the increase of value is specific to just basmati rice or few other products as waiting or stocking may not offer similar results for all products. It is an economic activity for sure but does not fit in modern production, distribution, consumption or exchange activities.

If above incident of economic nature does not fall in any of the four conventional classes then what is it for them i.e., when the rice is neither sold further nor is consumed as yet? One may say, stocking is a sub-class of distribution category, that's okay with another level of category but why the two, stocking and distribution, are called or labeled as classes of economic activities? There must be some inner reason common in them as *economic activity*. In our concept, the '*changing value*' or the '*change of value*' is the reason central to all *economic activities* whatsoever and where the prime mover of the change in value is only the *nature*, *man* or *machine*. The difference thus is – conventional system does not claim any internal reason common in their given categories and neither it accepts the role of *nature* in creating or amending value and leaves these activities without any place in their thoughts but here we do.

Example 2

The *change of value*, recognized by the difference of exchange-values at the input and the output, can occur either way i.e., either the difference is positive denoting profit or negative implying the loss. In first example, the change was positive caused by nature over a period of time in basmati rice; quite the opposite, a decrease in value occurs by nature in perishable products that reduces the worth of produce by the passage of time; at times the falling worth goes to a level that the owner of perishable produce may not even recover the value of its labour alone and possibly to get nothing as a result of this value descending process. In our scheme this is a diminution type of *economic activity*, but there is no equal thought exists for this happening in conventional narrative of *economic activity*.

Example 3

Another merit point of distinction in our thinking on the subject of economic activity vis-à-vis conventional thinking is the function of trading; in our draft, trading is a typical activity relevant to three classes except the creation of value category (*obviously because the article of trade must be existing before it can be traded, existence is when created*). Since we are employing the reason of 'changing value' for the definition of economic activity, therefore it also implies that there is always a life of an exchange value (*such life formative causes can be many including but not limited to natural, perceptive or enforced by market dynamics*); with every *change of value* that occurs, previous *exchange value life* is expired and new *exchange value life* is started that may keep on repeating unless the *exchange value* becomes zero. Owing to our reason of definition applied to the activity of trading, it is rationally understandable that the same economic product may be traded with real advantage if the value is increased (i.e., *the condition of profit, augmentation*), without change in the value ab-intra (*transference*) or by incurring loss (*diminution, consumption*).

2.6 Financing Correlation of new classes

In the philosophy of coherences, if a basic coherence is established for its reasons in a subject of belief, then it may generate, put or derive other coherences to fall in right pots. The coherent reason of '*changing value*' to define *economic activity* and new classification scheme on the bases of the reason, creates a logical coherence of linkage between the types of financings as well i.e., the suitability of a *financing form* for a particular class of *economic activity*, that we can show here as:

Table 2 : Correlation of New Classes

Economic Activity Type	*Suitable Financing Type*
Creation	: Logically Equity
Augmentation	: Equity and Loan
Transference	: Loan and Debt
Diminution	: Debt only

The economic significance of this parallel is more than just the correlation; for a balanced or progressive economy, an objective contribution of all four classes is required; if any national economy is dominated by the last two activities (i.e., *transference* and *diminution*), certainly then, it will lead the nation to debts, poverty and negative trade of balance.

3. Forms of Financing

As expected, an *economic activity* will require some *economic input(s)* to put into the *economic process* for the required purpose; it's also possible that there may exist an actual or intentional deficit of *economic input(s)* to begin the process; if such is the case, the sponsors of *economic activity* will seek external sources to deal with the insufficiency. If deficient inputs are acquired by mutual agreements with their owners/providers, the *economic activity* can be carried out and the job is done. However, it's not always practical or convenient, for many reasons possible with the owners of the property, sponsors of the activity or even by the *economic process* itself, that an association or partnership be formed. Normally, external sources would agree to supply what they can offer but may not show their willingness to become partner in the *economic activity*; therefore their properties can be acquired lawfully at their terms, usually by means of exchanging with money – the most doable option in practice generally. The sponsor(s) of *economic activity* may also face some deficit in setting up the economic process as well. Logically, for all such shortages on the part of activity sponsor(s), it is always sensible and convenient for them to seek and deal with a single source i.e., a finance provider to acquire his property (*money*) in the first place and then manage the rest of deficiencies with it. Obviously, dealing with a single source instead of making several contracts for the supply of other inputs discretely, is preferable. The '*forms of financings*' are the naturally possible basic arrangements with a finance provider for the purpose.

In view of the fact that, primarily we are discussing the contractual subject of financing here and not any specific economic process, precisely therefore our main and focal economic input is the money as a contractual concern of the contract. The real economic inputs are too many that is not even possible to list here. In order to simplify economic inputs, we may divide all possible *economic inputs* to an activity in two groups, i.e., one as '*money inputs*' and the rest as '*other inputs*'.

In a financing contract established for a purpose, we may obviously expect concerns and roles of entities be defined in the agreement finalized between them. The concerns are primarily related to the transactions of money (flow of money) and the target of profit. We can portray an overall spectrum of such possible flows of economic inputs to or from sponsors and financiers to go through the process to the close of the contract.

Interestingly, the type of input, the source of input and flow route of *economic input* naturally corresponds to one basic form of financing i.e., two types of inputs (money, other), the sources of inputs (financier or the sponsor) and from where to where makes a basic form of financing recipe. The correlation of input types and its route as resulting in the basic form of financing may be tabulated as below:

Table 3 : Flow of Economic Inputs

Type of input	Flow of economic input from	Financing Form
Money	*Finance provider to Economic Activity*	Equity
Money	*Finance provider to Sponsor*	Loan
Money	*Finance provider to an intermediary or on-purpose Economic Activity*	Debt
Money	*Sponsor to Economic Activity*	Equity
Money	*Sponsor to an intermediary or on-purpose Economic Activity*	Debt
Other Inputs	*Finance provider through on-purpose economic activity to main Economic Activity*	Debt

The sponsor is the 'activity doer' actually. In graphic form, the above flow of *economic inputs* to *economic activity* is shown in figure 4:

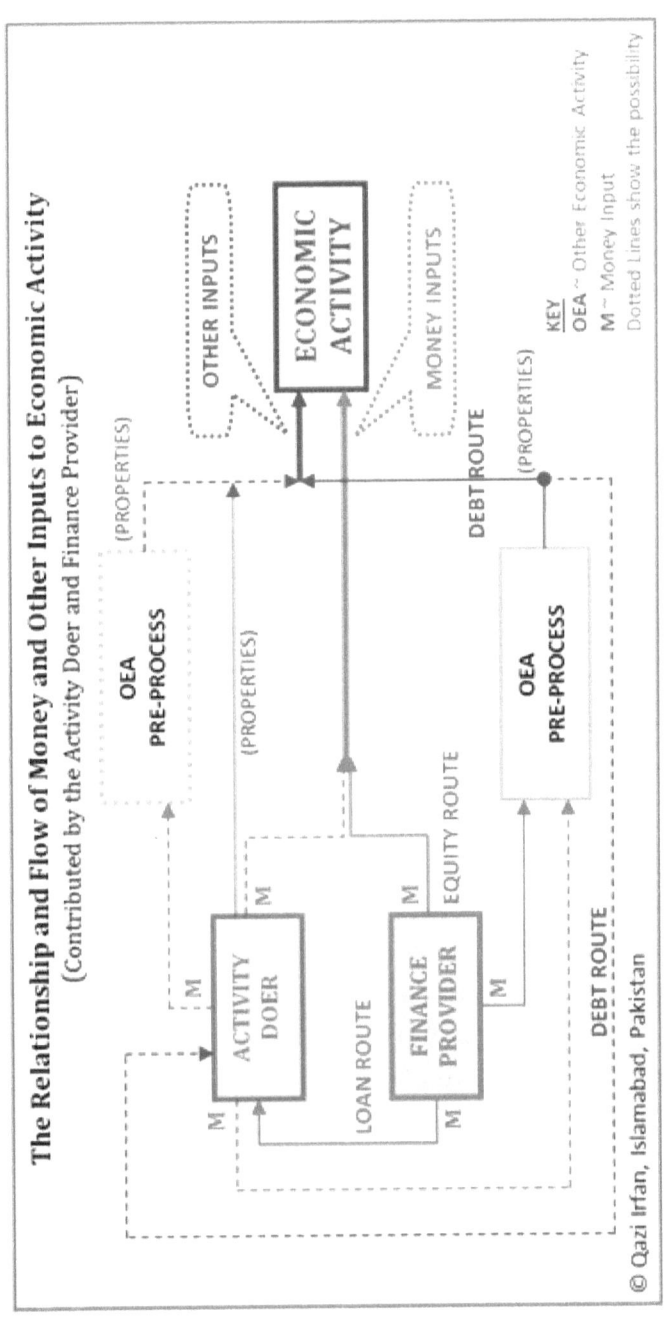

Figure 4 : Financing Forms

73

The figure shows the entire spectrum of possibilities for the flow of money and other inputs to an economic activity. All money routes indicated above are possible financing forms resulting in different types of contract. These routes are logical options for the financing of an economic activity. Since financing is predominantly ruled by the laws of nature, therefore every probable option is a natural option and every option is subject to the natural law of profit if to be used for making profit.

We may not forget that the involvement of 'finance provider' is indeed based on his motive of profit; thus any of three basic identified routes shown in the figure above (i.e., equity, loan and debt routes) may be agreed with the financier to meet his motive of profit i.e., the financing form is selected at the stage of *economic input*. Based on the form of financing selected, further role or concerns of finance provider will be defined naturally in the *economic process* or subsequent matters. Next we will address such natural concerns of finance provider.

If economic activity being financed is also planned for making profit from it, then the motives of sponsor and the finance provide will coincide naturally; most of the activities in 'creation and augmentation' categories offer such synchronization. On the other hand, if the intended economic activity falls within 'transference or diminution' category then motives of the two are not harmonized. This is a significant distinction in our way of thinking that creates a correlation between the forms of financings and the types of economic activities.

All activities that are not intended for making profit from it or the activity in itself does not offer a positive change of value to incur ab-intra (*from within the activity*), then the activity cannot offer profit to the finance provider as well (e.g. consumption); in such cases, 'Debt Route' is the only natural and suitable way for a 'for-profit' purpose. The finance provider, instead of giving his money to the sponsor, may use his money to submit 'other input' i.e., property to the activity; in this way he can construct his profit in the property he is submitting to the activity, or you can say that the finance provider used his money in an on-purpose pre-process economic activity (OEA) in order to produce required property (*OEA is an altogether separate and isolated activity*). Logically, the debt route of financing is natural option under 'transference and diminution' categories of economic activities where the resultant *exchange value* of '*economic output*' does not offer a gain.

The economic activity planned to make profit from it, implies that the expected exchange value of output is greater than the exchange value of input (e.g., a trading activity of real advantage, value addition activities of all sorts etc.) can rightly be financed by 'Loan' and 'Equity' forms of financing. However, using 'Debt' form (i.e., by putting property or non-money input) to such profit seeking activities is also possible and may not be ruled out completely (*because Equity through Debt is a possible blended form*). Practically, a form of financing or even a blended form, agreed upon for a profit making activity, is principally a matter of willingness or the possibility of the 'involvement degree' of the finance provider in that economic activity.

The degree of involvement of every partaker in the activity shall be an open subject to be decided mutually between them. The role of any partaker in the activity can be anything – from none to some, or from none to whole or exclusive, obviously they can move forward only with some agreement on this subject since no one can deny the involvement of other in the activity.

Accordingly, there can be any role for the finance provider as agreed with the sponsors of the activity; the reason is his motive of profit and bringing in his money to do the activity. The concerns of finance provider and the sponsors of the activity starting from the economic process to the return of money (close of activity) are undeniable on any pretext except if agreed mutually.

In next figure though, only the concerns of finance provider are outlined discretely for each of three forms of financing (shown inside dotted gray block).

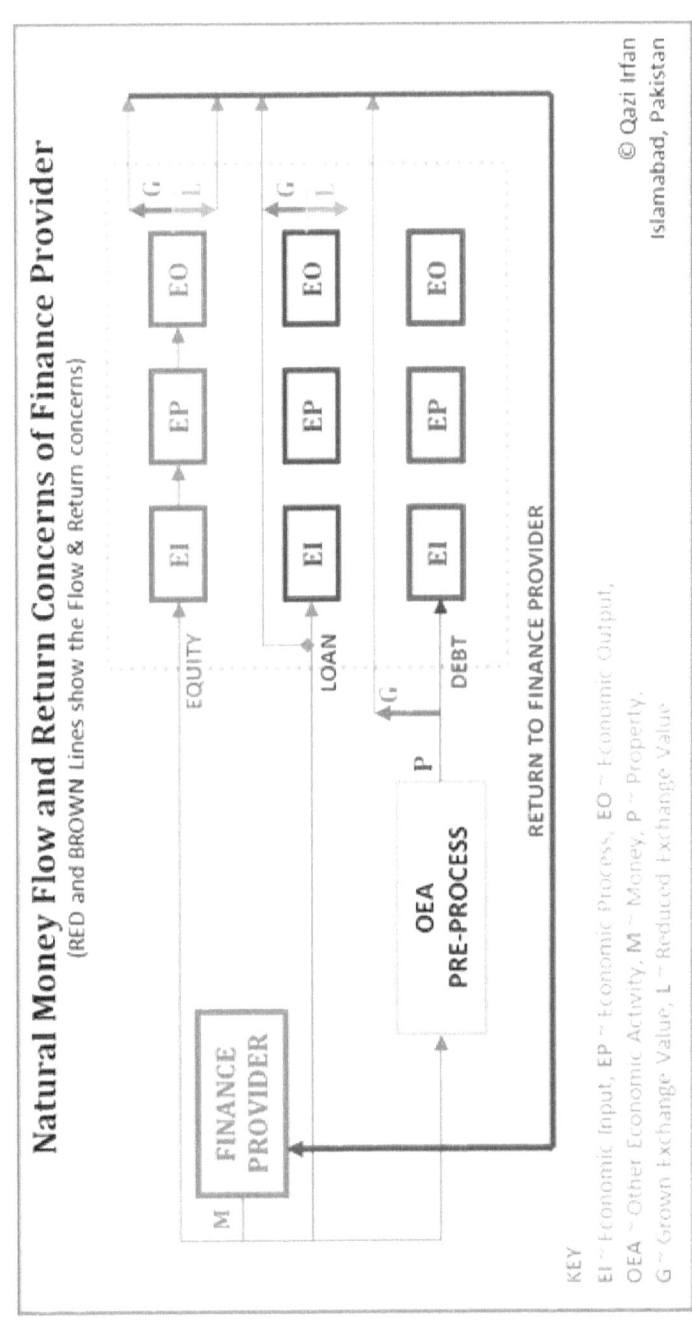

Figure 5 : Money Flow and Concerns

As shown in the figure above, the finance provider would certainly have built his profit while opting to finance the activity through Debt arrangement i.e., he has created a payment liability on the sponsors having no concerns ahead in the economic activity as a whole since his profit is defined at this stage. Other than the Debt arrangement, the finance provider may have real concerns in economic inputs (EI), economic process (EP), and economic output (EO) owing to fact that his profit is not yet defined and he has brought his money to finance the activity to have some profit from it. Such natural concerns of finance provider are inherent and undeniable.

The active role of individual partaker in managing the activity may be agreed between them mutually, to get engaged in economic process together and divide or assign responsibilities and operations between them by agreement. One may trust the other by allowing him to execute the activity on his behalf (i.e., *by giving him the rights to execute; by accepting the results*) or may reach any other effective agreement between them to bear the liability of the activity jointly with its consequences. If any of above arrangements is made between them with mutual consent, this agreement will imply a joint undertaking of the economic activity and therefore the contract will be 'Equity type' in essence – they are now jointly responsible of the whole activity and also for the outcome from it either be it a benefit or loss.

If no role or liability is determined for the finance provider in economic process (economic activity) for any reasons whatsoever (including his willingness or his lack of capability), then this will be a situation not the same as above; in this case logically, he shall not be held responsible for any loss by design or by force since he took no direct or indirect liability of the process, and at the same time his concern to any value gain in the economic output must be accepted by default for very obvious reason of supplying his money in expectation of some gain from the activity. If failure to construct a gain from the activity is resulted, it shall be the sole liability of the activity doer given that he was executing the process. In moral, realistic and rational economic thinking, the money-input provided by the financier shall be protected by the law for its preferential return or as agreed mutually. Yet, if profit is realized, then the finance provider shall have his due share per mutual agreement of sharing the profit. This is straightforward 'Loan' arrangement in a 'for profit' financing deal.

Summing up the concerns of finance provider in all three modes of financing, we may review the facts with natural tendencies. It's obvious that if an on-purpose pre-process economic activity is set out to facilitate few inputs to economic activity other than the money, then the two activities must be treated as separate events principally. Therefore, the finance provider literally has no concern to the internal dynamics of the economic activity he is financing through debt. Logically because, a *Ready Input* to an economic activity is an output from a former economic activity that's already concluded and cannot have any relation to this economic activity as an activity. If we summarize, the natural concerns of finance provider are just following three:

1. If, his motive of 'profit' is achieved by carrying out a provisional activity to contribute in current economic activity, then he has no concern ahead in the process or dynamics of economic activity.

2. However if above is not the case, obviously then, his motive of 'profit' can only be realized when economic output (EO) is determined; therefore his concerns are obvious till the time such results are defined. This is the state of *limited concerns* only related to the economic output.

3. No concern is the first state, limited concern is second and *full concern* is the third state starting from his involvement in putting up his money, through the process to the economic output i.e., from start to the close of the event.

On the other hand, the natural concerns of finance provide at different stages of an economic activity in view of the forms of financing, are:

1. In Equity form, his concerns are EI, EP, and EO.

2. In Loan form, these are only EI & EO.

3. In Debt form, he has no concern at all to the current activity.

However, in prevailing conventional practices, these natural concerns are camouflaged that is shown in next section i.e., handling of financing forms.

3.1 Handling of Financing Forms

It is expected of two doctrines (i.e., conventional and Islamic) to have different ways of handling or dealing with money, but the matter of fact is that two of three fundamental forms i.e., 'Debt' and 'Equity', actually have no or little philosophical or notional differences (*however blended forms like diminishing Musharakah are not analogous*), whereas only 'Loan' form of financing have serious inflexible positions at odds in the two that we will discuss first; later while discussing the Islamic handling of these forms, will highlight general handling and neglect, and some food for thought as well.

Since primary difference of handling is in loan form, we may re-draw the previous illustration and mark the gain in loan spot as 'alienated part' that is common to both forms of financing, as shown in below figure:

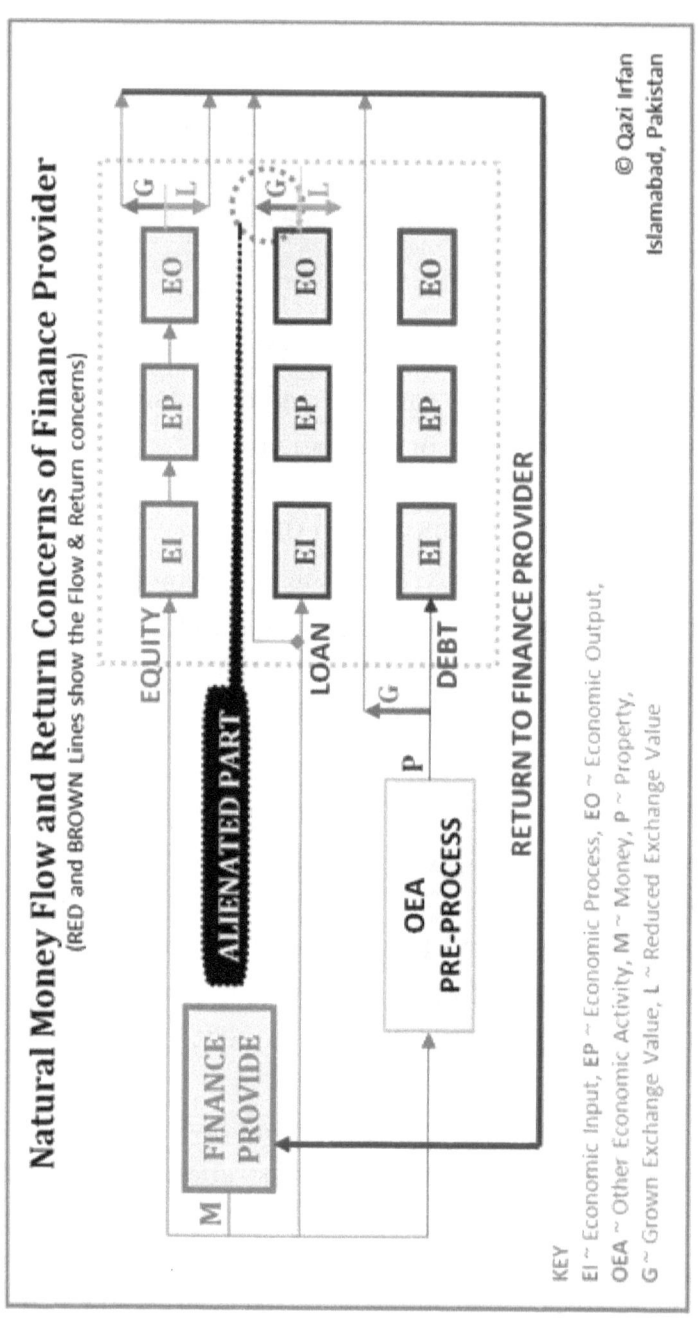

Figure 6 : Money Flow and Concerns - Alienated Part

This 'Alienated Part' is the most complex component earning all sorts of differences amid two doctrines and it's the primary source of conceptual confusions. If any practical separation of affairs, in two doctrines, is to be defined then this is the place, and analyzing respective handling of this ill-treated part can do that only.

Conventional System

The desire of 'profit' is not rejected in any system of belief; it is very natural and serves as catalyst in human interactions but the way it is enforced unnaturally in conventional financing is disappointing.

As per our novel definition of economic activity, the change of value occurs by some 'economic process', this change is available in the 'economic output' having an 'exchange value' with three probabilities i.e., either the resultant 'exchange value' is more than the input value submitted (means profit is made) or less than that (i.e., loss incurred) or remained the same (i.e., no profit, no loss); only one of three state is possible in the outcome. These are natural possibilities having no fourth option to occur for the exchange-value of the outcome from an economic activity in anyway. Since our context here is 'financing for-profit' therefore we are not considering 'impact value' subjects. The natural possibilities must be handled naturally, let us first see the conventional handling of economic output (EO), as shown in below figure with its evident abuse of 'Loan' based activity.

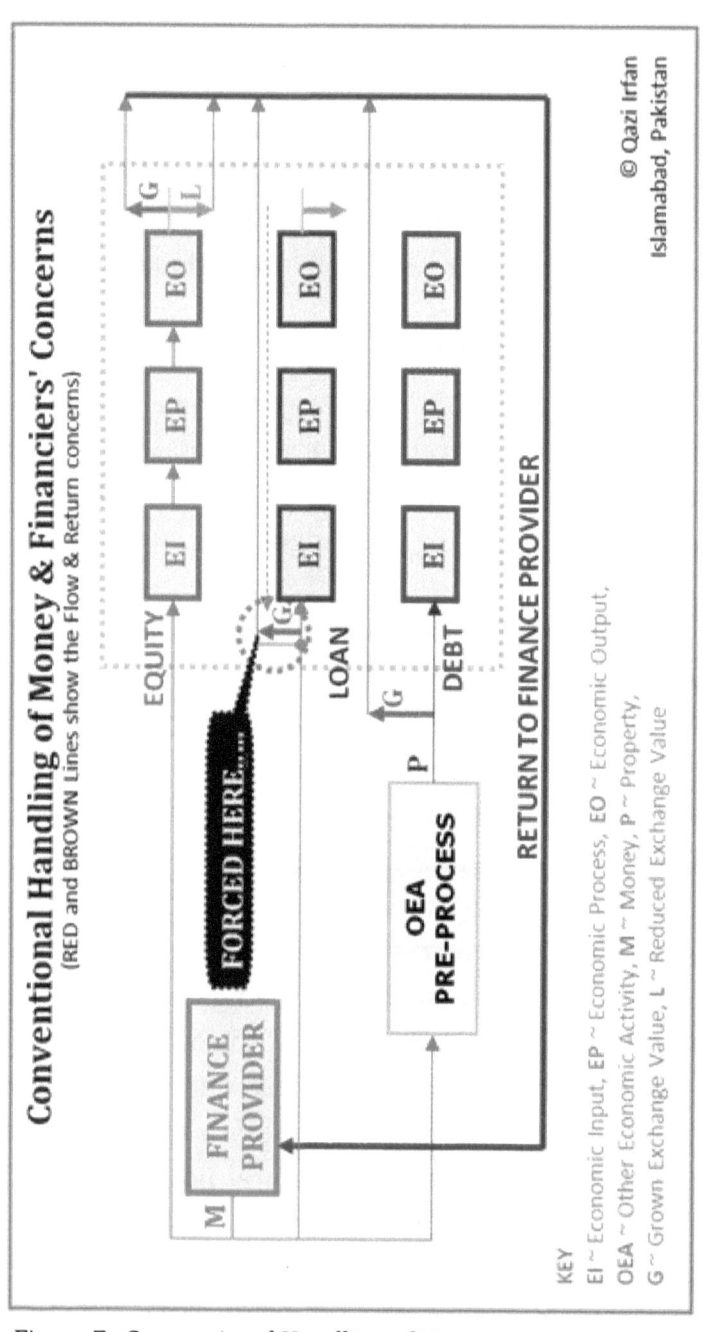

Figure 7 : Conventional Handling of Money

Above pictorial illustration of conventional handling speaks of itself; the earlier marked 'alienated part' is moved from its natural position to this forced position. The motive of profit is fair enough but the conventional approach has adopted an artificial course for defining and realizing it, forcing it to exist where it is not doable rather absolutely perverted. The 'Profit' does not and cannot exist at this stage of an economic activity which is precisely the argument for the non-existence of this excess element in a loan arrangement. Whatever name you give it – *Riba*, Usury, Interest, *Sood* or else, and wherever you go on earth and call for help to bring a credible justification for this act, there is no possibility that some one can prove the existence of 'Profit' at this point in an economic activity. Humanly developed laws are not eternal but this one is the law of the nature (for profit) that is not going to change anyway.

There is huge perceptive difference in two positions of 'Profit' – where it can exist and where it is forced to exist; whole conventional philosophy of making profit through loan financing arrangements is based on this lie or deception. Without any biased notion or narrow-mindedness or any kind of prejudice but in very honest view – such gain is not a natural and legal profit.

If we create 'cause and effect' analogy to the event of economic activity, then 'economic process (EP)' is the cause and 'economic output (EO)' is its effect that may hold 'Profit'; how an effect can be acknowledged prior to its cause? The conventional conduct is eager not only to change the natural law of profit but other norms and philosophies without having any of its own logic or reasoning but through the use of force only.

Islamic Handling

In our belief, Islam is consistent with nature[8] – this essential religious convention is applicable to the law of profit as well. We must also recognize that Islam and Islamic understanding are two different things; Islam is eternal and perfect (*belief*) but Islamic understanding is the reflection and thinking of fallible human beings thus impermanent and may be imperfect. In prevailing thinking (*Islamic Fiqh*), though the position of profit is not moved in an economic activity as the conventional proponents do, however current Islamic thinking has another kind of fallacy about profit in loan financing.

Next illustration shows the Islamic handling of loan form of financing; in the loan band of activity, there is no connection between the profit element and return path of money. The profit is **ignored here** by labeling it unlawful (*haram*) without any valid reason in Islamic doctrine (*Shariah*); a valid concern of finance provider is rejected, why? Thus, in a profit generating economic activity, loan is not workable mode in prevalent Islamic law and this is of course due to the confusion on *Riba*.

---

[8] *Quran 30:30*

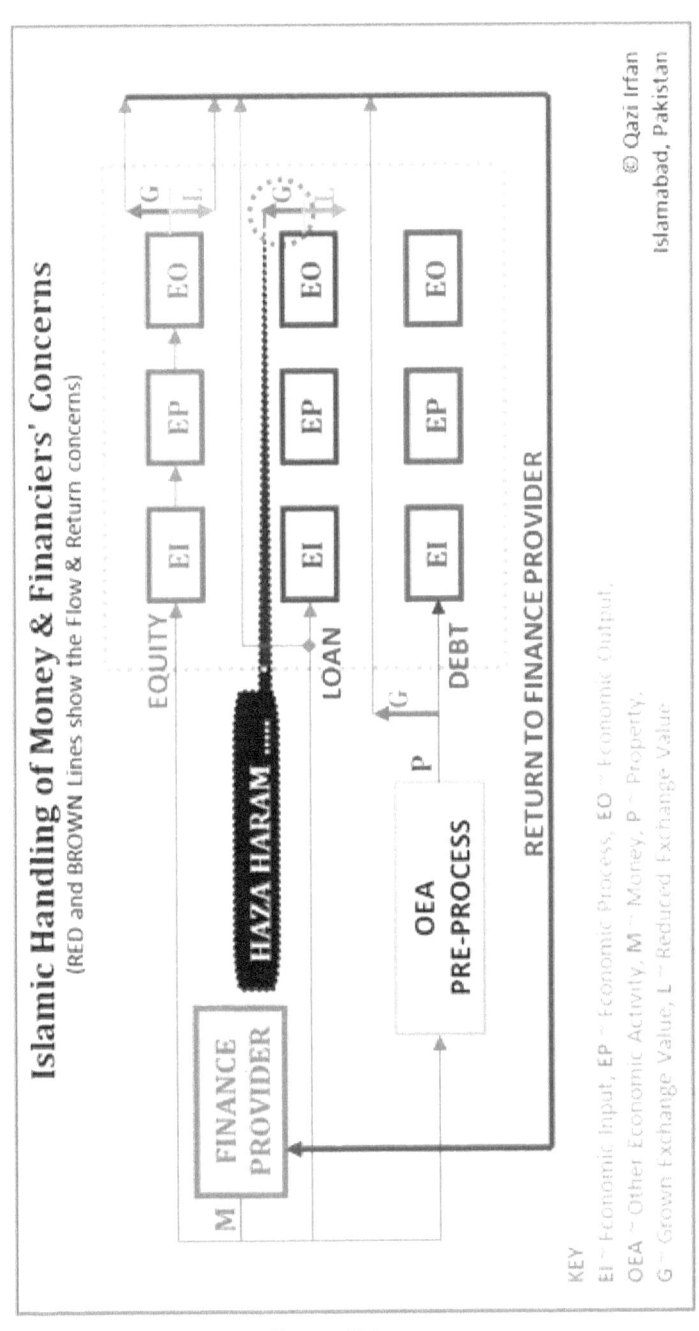

Figure 8 : Islamic Handling of Money

87

The worst part is that neither the confusion is done away nor the existing law is adhered to; means you are doing what you think is not lawful. This is because you cannot ignore profit at its natural place of existence. It is the natural way of earning profit, therefore in Islamic money practices, profit is not ignored here but strange theories are created to overcome this dichotomy of law and practice. The artificial theories or imitated ideas of ingenuity, in today's practices, to cover up the fault of law are not convincing. Instead, the use of tricky and imprudent ideas as opposed to traditional *Islamic* way of handling the subjects, has in fact further intensified the confusion; for instance, the 'deposits' received by Islamic banks (*from customers who are their finance providers*) are treated exactly like 'Loan' arrangements but are labeled with other pretended forms so that the law is not considered been violated (*unnatural thinking but natural working; conflicting thinking and working*).

If we go a bit more in details of this perplexity i.e., the Islamic stance about loan vis-à-vis the practice of taking deposits, then we may see that in order to justify the practice of taking deposit but not accepting it loan, obviously the proponents of current Islamic finance need to have some other concept or philosophy to label this 'taking of deposit' instead of calling it loan – there they have options like *Qard Hasan, Wadiah, Amanah*[9]

---

[9] *Benevolent loan (money lent but no terms of return and no benefit), safe keeping, the trust based holding or keeping of one's assets*

etc., but unfortunately none of these known Islamic concepts comply with the practice of taking deposit as the original meanings and conditions of these terms do not allow; this mismatched situation translates into the fact that we are trying to alter the sense and meanings of previously established concepts. The casual conduct of contemporary Islamic banking professionals seems eager to change the glorious well-known models and philosophies forcibly; will manipulation of previously indisputable norms would protect the valuable *Fiqh* and *Shariah* or will distort it consequently?

If we assume that this false labeling is not false but a real and modern Islamic way of doing business, then the Islamic banks and financial institutions must also approve and extend these methods to their customers who are seeking money i.e., same terms of *Qard Hasan*, *Wadiah*, and *Amanah* as their regular financing modes. The truth is, this is not happening both ways but in one way only i.e., to get money from depositing customers. Previously, these concepts and operations were in use well before the banking or Islamic banking was started. A pathetic argument is given frequently that the society is so corrupt that people cannot be trusted or at least banks cannot trust people and thus the same practice cannot be extended to public. Is it really the case? How societies can exist with total corruption where banks are also part of it? These are all feeble excuses, showing greedy conventional mentality and assumptions that are not even tested; we don't see angels from heaven sitting in the banks as well.

As against to natural concerns of finance provider in a 'Loan' type financing – if the conventional handling of profit is forced and misleading then the Islamic handling of profit is irrational and depressing too; both orthodox handlings are abnormal and strange, a revisit to the subject by both is required to correct and align it with nature.

In view of the natural law of profit and in addition to the valid and undeniable concerns of finance provider in a profit generating activity; we offer few challenges to the advocates of Islamic banking and finance for the dilemma faced by them i.e., thinking vis-à-vis practice, while dealing with profit in loan financing, as below:

1.   Loan arrangement in a 'For Profit' financing of economic activities is **not allowed**, yet it is **practiced one way**, therefore some out-of-box and bravery thinking effort is required from Islamic scholars to legitimize the unidirectional ongoing practice on purely realistic and natural lines in order to remove the confusion?

2.   Since profit is not treated correctly at its natural place within conventional methodology (*i.e., where it can exist*) therefore no such work or knowledge, skills or practices, tactics or technology is readily available to

Islamic operations that can be useful for expected and proper handling of the profit at its right place. That is to say, conventional handling of loan arrangements is artificial and by force, that is not workable for Islamic handling if it goes with real profit in loan form.

3.   A loan and loan based financing (i.e., protected investment) are surely not the same type of contracts because of intentions. If contemporary *Shariah* scholars ever approve loan based financing 'For Profit' motives (*by removing present confusion in thinking and practices*), then there is a huge task ahead to develop methodical handling of **profit** at its correct place where it exists in an economic activity; a fresh dimension of knowledge & technology shall come to reality that will certainly be different from present-day tools and techniques used in conventional practices e.g., like for deal evaluation, customer profiling, profit determination, managing the risk elements, auditing and other standards etc. This will definitely be seen as a different kind of banking than conventional or present Islamic banking.

Owning to the dilemma of rejecting profit altogether in a loan form of financing i.e., not accepting loan form of financing as a valid Islamic operation to make profit, the religious financial technologists are altering other model contracts of Islamic jurisprudence to imitate the conventional loan financing method and believing that they are making an equity contract. For instance, the so-called 'equity' financing instrument developed by modern Islamic minds i.e., diminishing *Musharakah*, is flawed at the root and this derivative of well known *Musharakah* contract has indeed damaged the Islamic model contract. Let me further explain and clarify how the label of *Musharakah* is misused pitifully – 'equity' is when profit is to come from the outcome of economic activity; 'debt' is when profit is built in economic input before the activity has taken place; in this diminishing *Musharakah* imitator, the profit is already included in the price of the property, divided into shares that are gradually transferred to the customer by reducing the ownership stake of financier in the property, eventually making his part to become zero (to exit from the deal). No profit has to come from the outcome. Therefore, the modern so-called Islamic diminishing *Musharakah* is a debt form of financing and since the debt is created by investing the money hence it is a loan not equity.

In fact, there is no possibility to establish an 'equity' form of financing, to make profit from transference or diminution type of activities, only debt form is possible in such cases. The diminishing partnership hypothesis fabricated in property ownership is utterly fake and false – just by owing something cannot be considered as partnership in an economic activity, this mechanism can merely provide security for the repayment of debt. It is observed further that this false understanding of ownership theory is irrationally employed to justify an insupportable thinking when it is said that to *Shariahfy* a transaction, if constructive ownership of subjective substance is kept momentarily only, it is OK. Alas! The minds go off as to understand what is that? Why is that? And how is that even conceived in the first place?

Practically, instead of adding some value to *Shariah* heritage of *Fiqh*, we are destroying it. We are our own adversary, foolish friends. There are many examples of misunderstanding the work of our predecessors by the modern thinking minds, for instance, taking another misread of *Modarabah* contract i.e., the condition that if a loss is incurred in this joint venture (of equity), the finance provider (*Rub-ul-maal*) will bear it alone; there is another condition that finance provider have no role in managing the business. In our contemporary wise scholarship, these contractual terms or conditions are taken as *de facto* principles or rules i.e., not recognizing the fact of difference in principles and terms; principles are obligatory to follow in all sorts of contracts while terms are specific to some particular situations.

Our contemporary scholars have derived a principle from a terms that loss will always be attributed to the finance provider; this ingenious and so-called *Shariah* ruling is derived from a contract of partnership, from specific terms and conditions designed for a particular situation where activity doer (*Mudarib*) had nothing to put in the economic activity and financier had no intent or capability to participate in the activity. It was a demand of justice that if *Mudarib* discharges his task with honesty and responsibility but loss incurs then he would not be made liable for the loss since he had no capacity to bear the loss. The contract of *Modarabah* has extensive sense and business concept in it. Now, leaving the framework out of sight, they have made it a rule that all losses shall always be borne by the finance provider regardless of any situation. Moreover, joining this misread with another misread from another model contract; since finance provider cannot take part in the *Modarabah* activity but unless his counterpart does not put some finance in it, where in that case the contract is not *Modarabah* but *Musharakah*.

Owning to deducted rules, you can offer *Modarabah* even to those who have no need for an external finance and have enough of their own money to carry out the economic activity, also you cannot demand or have a role or control in the activity – how dangerous and risky that business would be inherently when financed out of contextual situation for which it was meant? If the sponsors of economic activity are reluctant to use their own finance in their intended activity, then the business must be highly risky and it would be quite unfair with finance provider to assume all risk alone. The concept of *Modarabah* is entirely tarnished. These alleged *de facto* rules are basically the most significant and primary cause in the failure of *Modarabah* ventures financed by Islamic banks and financing institutions as were tried and enforced to situations where they could not fit and were not designed for. On the other hand, just because of the *de facto* deducted rules, many valid opportunities are not entertained but rejected.

The set of terms (or even if you take terms as rules) that are defined for respective situations of *Modarabah* and *Musharakah* are different, which itself is a proof of the argument that terms (or rules if you say it so) are made for situation and not otherwise. If a situation is changed then to do the justice, a new set of terms and conditions can be applied to that particular situation of economic interaction.

The earlier noble Islamic scholars of *Shariah* or *Fiqh* were able to deal successfully with any situation that was put to them seeking to develop a model contract of conduct; their key concerns have always been to build justice, prevent exploitation, protect rights of involved parties, adhere to religious tenets etc. in designing the contract with clear definitions of terms and conditions for that particular situation.

However, the *Modarabah* and *Musharakah* or other model contracts defined by earlier scholars, may not imprison *Shariah* within the context of agreements they developed even partly; model contracts are not more than just validated by *Shariah* for explicit situation. The validation shall be limited to the pertinent situation only, principally.

In reality, there are several situations that were not handled by them previously simply for the reasons that those situations were not existing at that time (e.g., like the one emerged after the inclusion of intermediaries within financing practices). The current situations are inviting recent *Shariah* experts to develop new conduct models (contracts) properly, but I have a suggestion for modern Islamic Financial Technologists of any stature – if they are unable to handle the 'untreated situations' with same motif of contract development as our former Islamic scholars used to do, then they should at least keep their brains and hands off of previous works for the sake of preserving the legacy rather than destroying it by their poor work.

What is a situation or 'untreated situation'? This is a relevant query in view of above analysis and our topic of financing for profit. As stated above that a situation is developed by the involvement of intermediaries, this situation was not treated in available *Fiqh*, therefore we call it an 'untreated situation'. Logically, a situation exists before it can be treated therefore any inference that is extracted from previous situation may not be applicable to current situation since the two situations are not the same. If we try to enforce same terms and conditions made for an earlier situation to a dissimilar current situation, then it will mean that we are trying to force the current situation to change; it is futile to create a situation from a contract (i.e., to enforce rules derived from *Modarabah* and *Musharakah* on different situations); if it is done than it will be a forced contract (misplaced and mishandled) that can destroy existing situation, generating a new situation, needing again to be handled amicably with a suitable new contract.

3.2 Spectrum of financing situations

The ingenious contemporary scholars have confined the whole extensive nature of financing interactions in few situations that were treated in early *Fiqh*; curtailing the nature is like going against it. While the truth is, there are too many valid situations that may require an external finance since there are plenteous *factors and variables* (elements) that can define a unique situation.

Using these situation making elements, if we enlist and tabulate a basic recipe of factors and variable that can define a possible situation then we can see which combinations were treated earlier and which are not treated hitherto. Though, we considered only two types of input variables (money and other, ref to 'figure 4') to an economic activity however we can segregate inputs in as many variables as possible just by decomposing the properties of 'other inputs', if need to expand. The basic recipe of factors and variables is listed here just to understand basic possible situations:

Table 4 : Spectrum of Financing Situations

Factors	Variables
Economic Inputs	Money Properties Human Work
n x Activity Doer(s)	with/without Money with/without Properties Human Work
n x Financier(s)	with/without Money with/without Properties with/without Human Work
n x Economic Activity(ies)	Economic Inputs n x Economic Processes n x output(s)

(Note - Here above, 'n' means 'one or more')

Next, if we include the intentions and capabilities of the participants i.e., owners and mediators like banks; their undeniable and negotiable rights, and their valid natural concerns etc. etc., just imagine! How many combination of above variables are possible with these sensitivities, I can't put it here, perhaps we may need a computer program to do that.

For instance there might be a new situation like - if a financier has the intent and the capability to assume some role or control in a business and the activity doer agrees to his participation in the execution of economic activity while the activity doer is not investing any of his own finance in this joint venture, then it is neither a *Modarabah* situation nor the one like *Musharakah*; why it cannot be treated differently within a new contract by definition and on what grounds the situation can be rejected if we see beyond *Fiqh* resources, where else in *Shariah* such rejection is seen except barred by these *not credible de facto rules* deduced from contracts that do not fit in this situation?

A sole combination of available factors and variables will define a unique kind of situation (certainly before handling the situation, every element of combination shall pass through the filter as applicable for its *Islamic* permissibility), a contract for the valid unique situation can be made for the motive of 'profit' under discussion just by considering the following dynamics:

1. The circumstances of the participants and the Natural Law of Profit – A must dynamic to be observed to define the situation for profit.

2. Relevant tenets of Islamic doctrine (*Shariah*) as applied for the transactional procedures.

That's all, we have a tailored new contract – *Shariah* validated and this is very modest and realistic Islamic thinking.

The idea of *Diminishing Musharakah* is a typical case of discrepancy and inconsistency in current practices of modern Islamic banking and finance industry and their projected thinking on the subject. The confinement of Islamic philosophy of economic interactions in so small latitude of few contracts by our contemporary scholars is damaging the face of divine doctrine, a re-examining of these subjects is inevitable rather mandatory on the part of modern Islamic scholars and intellectuals so as to harmonize the *thinking with practice* or *practice with thinking* whatever is more realistic and acceptable as a result of the rework. Rather than removing the known confusion on *Riba* and its allusion, more confusion is introduced by the substandard work of contemporary scholars who are helping modern Islamic banking and finance industry; and which is also destroying earlier concepts where we had no confusion previously. It is very difficult to accept such truths.

4. Set of Terms

There are numerous concerns and modalities that are required to be addressed in a contract based on any form of financing. These are open subjects and can't be fixed by few thoughts and rulings; a progressive and realistic method is required in defining 'set of terms'. A partial and common list of concerns is appended below that are or could be the general topics under the terms and conditions:

Table 5 : Set of Terms

Subjects of Concern	Explanation or Sense
Principal Amount	Money contributed by respective finance provider(s)
Return or Settlement	Money payable to respective finance provider(s) and/or sponsors, partners, activity doer(s) or else
Profit	Increase (gain) over and above Principal Amount
Loss	Decrease (drop) below Principal Amount
Risk	The probability of losing Principal Amount, Return, and the uncertainty of realizing Profit
Use of Money	The way and means of spending money; the type of economic activity where money is employed
Payments	How the money will be repaid in fixed, flexible, periodic or relative to something, and time schedule for money for changing hands, either way
Security, Collateral	Counterpart's property; a way of managing the risk

Liabilities	Of working, managing, and ensuring the return of money, risk and loss
Ownership	Of properties (economic inputs, in setup of process and economic outputs)
Responsibilities	Of discharging commitments and implementing the tasks required in the process till closing of process
Sharing	Of responsibilities, working, liabilities, profit, loss, and/or risk
Time	Involvement at each stage and promise for investment, payments and use of money

Yet, the list is not exhaustive, there are plenty other concerns that may be added; particularly when some situation itself brings its own concerns to the economic activity being financed, e.g., need to monitor, evaluate, reassess, modify, improve, audit, quitting or exiting, expiring of an entity, default, transfer of ownership and responsibilities etc. etc. these are the conditions that might be considered and negotiated.

From above list of concerns, we may talk about three selected ones that are relatively more important to our topic of 'For Profit' financing i.e., Profit, Loss, and the Risk.

4.1 Profit, Loss & Risk

It is natural when we plan an economic activity for the purpose of profit, then at the stage of planning we may only estimate or desire what or how much profit we shall be making out of the activity. Therefore profit is an estimate initially. When economic activity is being executed then the actual dynamics of the process and operation will determine the magnitude of profit that is doable. Therefore in the second phase, profit is defined for its realistic size. The defined profit is not realized as yet unless the economic output is not sold to its buyer. Therefore, profit is realized when the proceeds of sale are effectively received.

If we consider 'Risk' as the probability of something that goes wrong in the whole process of profit or if we consider 'Risk' as a threat, danger or uncertainty in the way of profit; then by analogy of stages we can label or categorize risks for three stages respectively, as below:

1) Information risk at the stage of estimation.

2) Process or functional risk in execution phase.

3) Realization of profit risk in negotiation phase or concluding exchange.

Information risk, process risk, and realization risk are possible risky elements in all forms of financings; the basic risk spectrum is shown in figure below:

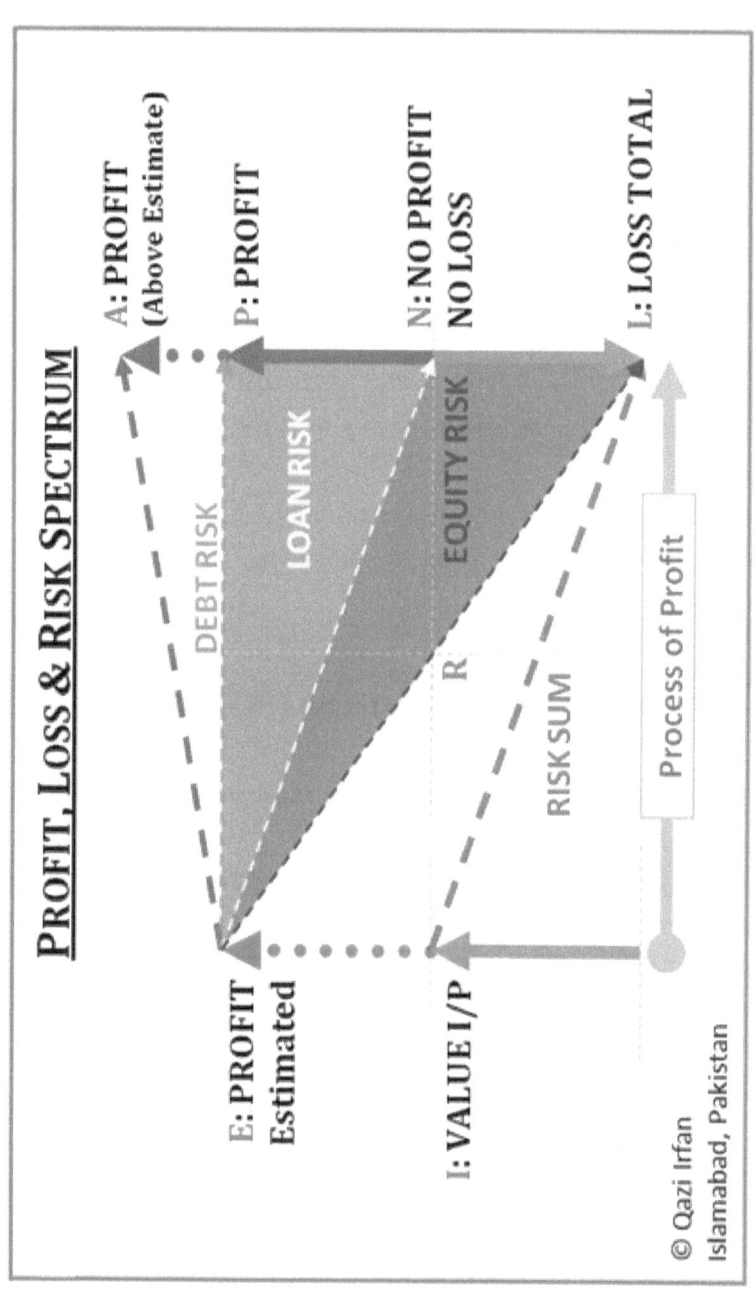

Figure 9 : The Risk Spectrum

The subject of risk is quite complex matter involving foreseen and unforeseen things; however risk spectrum figure shown above is fairly understandable as it says 'a picture is worth a thousand words'. It encircles all three forms of financings for the total probability of risk in each form. In the timeline of the 'process of profit', risk will always remain within the defined periphery of each mode of financing, whereas we may further translate elements of risk in many ways within its periphery.

The representation of risk sector for each financing mode is appended below along with the risk sum. Since the slope and delta depiction is different for each mode therefore respective contractual terms and condition shall be different as well. The variable profit direction indicate the probability of more profit than estimate in two modes (i.e., other than debt based financing).

Table 6 : The Risk Spectrum

Slope/Delta	*Risk Sectors in Forms of Financing*
E→P	Debt Risk (only Profit Realization Risk)
Δ EPN	Loan Risk (Partial Risk of Process i.e., Risk of Profit)
Δ EPL	Equity Risk (Full Risk of Process)
I→L	Risk Sum: (Total Risk of Surprise or Random nature)

The representation of risk is optimistically clear in my view and with a bit of my luck to my readers too. The risk, defined by slope/delta under equity, loan and debt labels is reasonably manageable for the concerns of involved entities; we may call it the 'foreseen' risks; however what is not within the knowledge, controlling capacity of involved entities or else reasons, is denoted by the 'Risk Sum', we may call it the 'unforeseen' risks. The floor point 'L' in the figure is the maximum effect of risk (total loss condition) in any form of financing; whereas the point 'P' represents the maximum gain as desired or doable profit and also the potential of taking or averting the risk. The point 'R' is for futuristic ideas.

We all agree that no one works for loss (i.e., against the motive) therefore it is only the factor of 'risk' that may cause a 'loss'; risk means the conditions that will swing between maximum effects of 'profit' and 'loss' in any phase i.e., estimation, process, and realization of profit. In relation to the forms of financing, 'estimation risk' and 'realization risk' are common to all forms of financings; whereas a part of process risk (i.e., risk in profit) is possible in 'loan form' and process risk in full obviously exist in 'equity form' of financing. Lastly, the 'risk sum' is something unknown that can do anything in any form without any bias. The handling of 'profit' is already discussed earlier; next let us see how Risk and Loss are handled in conventional and Islamic practices.

Conventional Handling of Risk

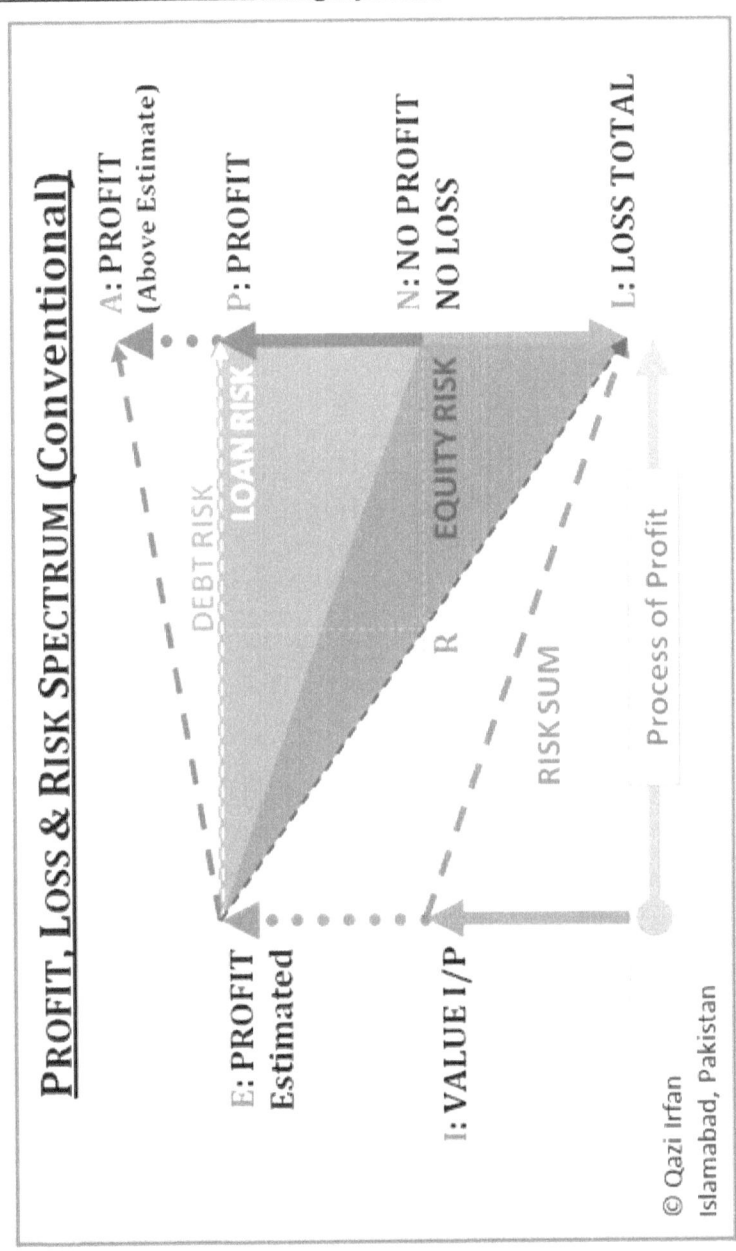

Figure 10 : Risk Spectrum - Conventional

The earlier figure of 'risk spectrum' is tailored above for conventional handling of risk per current financing practices. If we re-write earlier table of 'risk spectrum' accordingly, we may notice the change of 'loan delta' to 'debt slope' as per conventional loan financing practice.

Table 7 : Risk Spectrum - Conventional

Slope/Delta	Conventional Handling of Risk
E→P	Debt Risk (only Profit Realization Risk)
E→P IOF Δ EPN	Debt Risk Instead OF Loan Risk (~ only Profit Realization Risk)
Δ EPL	Equity Risk (Full Risk of Process)
I→L	Risk Sum: (Total Risk of Surprise or Random nature)

Unsurprisingly, there is no real 'loan risk handling' in conventional practices as they had forced the profit to exist artificially before it can, which means there is no partial risk of process (i.e., risk of profit) since profit is already fixed before the process. Virtually, there is no difference in conventional handling of risk in 'debt' and 'loan' forms. In practice, collateral is acquired to secure the debt or loan, in essence then the 'realization risk' is also not a risk, however, there could be extra efforts or expense required to recover the principal amount and the profit from the collateral. In any case though, the 'risk sum' of surprise or random nature is still there.

From any theoretical or practical point of view the probability of 'loss' in conventional handling of risk is almost negligible or non-existent. All loans and debts are generally secured against collateral pledged by the borrower and which is unexceptionally well more than the total payment liability created. Thus there is totally no possible contractual and transactional outcome that could affect the defined profit in conventional handling of 'foreseen' risk. It may be reiterated to reemphasize that conventional handling of loan and debt is the same and therefore the loan delta has been disappeared from the original 'risk spectrum' figure. In this perspective, we may conclude the 'conventional risk handling' as below:

Although, inherently the 'debt' and 'loan' forms of financings insist on having different handling terms to each form (this is because the slope and delta sectors in original 'risk spectrum' are distinctive), however since the so-called profit is forced to exist before it can really exist in a loan form of financing therefore the technical and contractual difference in two types of financings is demolished. The conventional handlers do not have different sets of 'risk measures' as required for the two forms of financings.

Islamic Handling of Risk

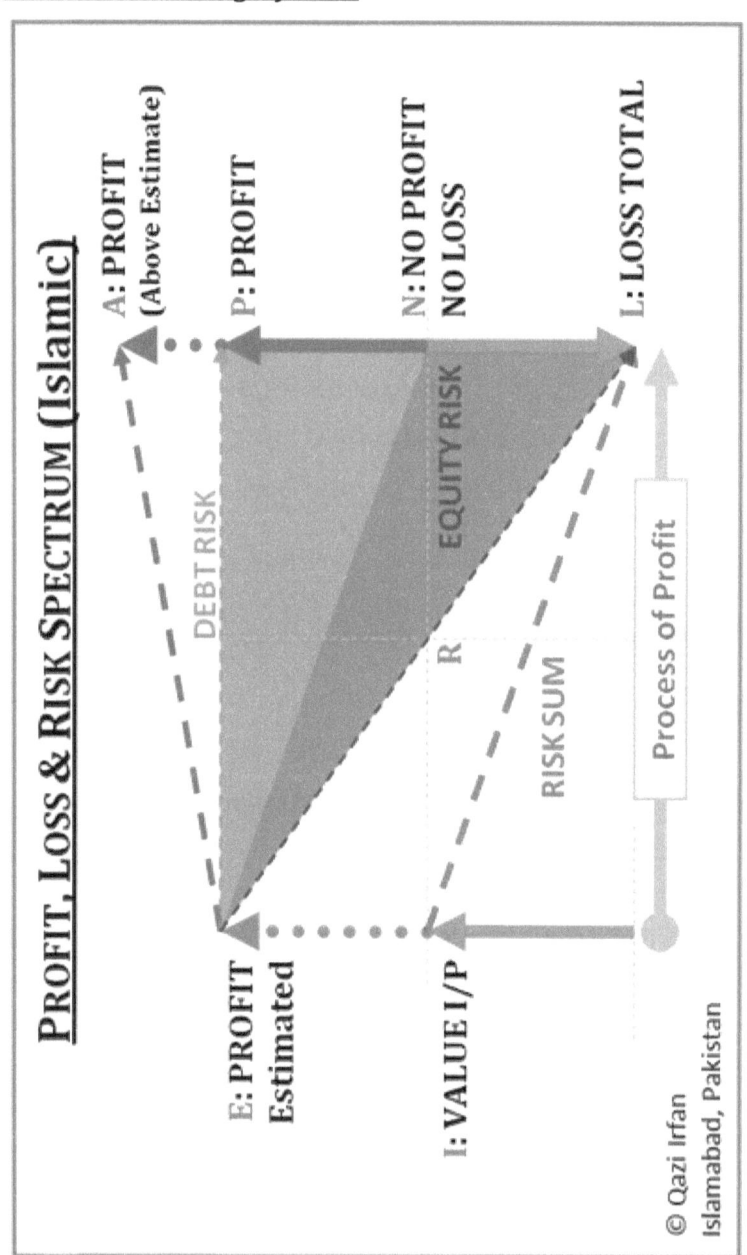

Figure 11 : Risk Spectrum - Islamic

In above modified figure of original 'risk spectrum' for Islamic handling of risk, we can see that there is no slope or delta referring to loan, accordingly let us make a table of risks as handled in Islamic operations for different forms of financings.

Table 8 : Risk Spectrum - Islamic

Slope/Delta	Islamic Handling of Risk
E→P	Debt Risk (only Profit Realization Risk)
EPN	No Loan 'For Profit' THUS No Loan Risk Probability (Delta disappeared)
Δ EPL	Equity Risk (or Risk of Principal plus Full Risk of Process)
I→L	Risk Sum: (Total Risk of Surprise or Random nature)

There is no handling of 'loan risk' in Islamic working because of the reason that theoretically the loan form of financing is not a legal form in Islamic finance today. Therefore, if you compare above figures and tables of risk spectrum for conventional and Islamic handlings, you will find that there is no difference except in loan form. Islamic handling of risk in the 'debt' and 'equity' modes is almost similar to the conventional handling throughout the process of profit, but differs only in the profit realization phase as we know and is evident by stipulated terms for late payments. The issue of penalty is a disputed matter in Islamic finance and related to the realization phase of profit as well.

Briefly, we may conclude on the handling of risk by the two doctrines, conventional and Islamic, that risk is treated almost the same way by both in debt and equity forms of financings; whereas in conventional loan form of financing, risk is treated just like as they do in debt form; whereas loan is not a legal form of financing in Islamic finance of today therefore corresponding risk in loan does not exist and that is not an issue in Islamic finance. The conventional and Islamic treatment of risk (or you can say the profit and loss conditions as well) are not logical and natural in loan form of financing as shown in our original risk spectrum.

•••

Murabaha Financing

Three fundamental forms of financings i.e., *debt*, *loan* and *equity* are inherently distinctive by definition. However, the conventional money system had buried the technical distinction between the 'debt' and 'loan' as the two are treated exactly the same way in practice. This concealment of distinction in their conduct was exposed by the launch of Islamic finance operations to contemporary money markets. The uncovering reason is that – the *Islamic* instrument of *Murabaha* financing devised by modern Islamic intellect is a 'debt' based instrument just like the conventionalists do; however since today's Islamic thinking altogether rejects any 'loan' financing agreement therefore this calls back the inherent difference between the debt and loan models. For conventionalists, if Islamists are doing debt based financings then why not loan based financings since for them there is no difference in the two. In this context, the query is to know the difference between 'Murabaha Financing and Lending on Interest'; the title of book is also derived from this primary query as well. There is no standing dissimilarity exists between conventional 'debt' and *Islamic Murabaha* financings at least to the point of defining the profit however it may and usually differs in the profit realization phase.

A few 'debt' based financing contracts are conceived in modern times using traditional contracts of Islamic jurisprudence i.e., *Murabaha, Bai Muajjal, Bai Bithaman Ajil* etc. Since *Islamic* model trade contracts are used to create debt based *Islamic* financing parallels, therefore we may consolidate them all in a basic debt structure for possible contractual terms. This all-inclusive debt model illustrates every general factor and the dynamics including the buyer, seller, financier, debt, commodity, deferment of payment, money and possible routes for the transfer of money and commodity.

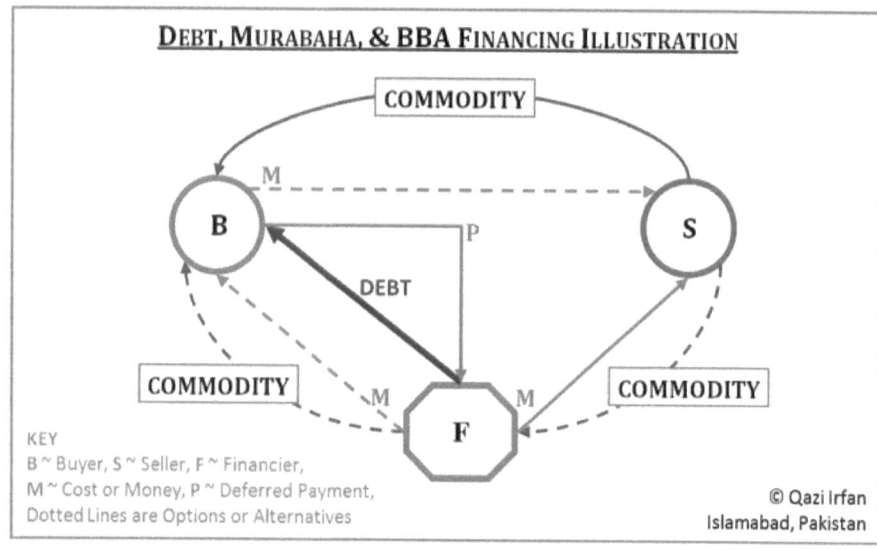

Figure 12 : Debt & Murabaha Structure

In above model obviously, a debt is must created on the buyer by each type of *Islamic* financing method that we have referred earlier. In the creation of 'Debt', the optional routes (shown by dotted lines) for the transfer of commodity or money are valid and justifiable means for the purpose of such transfers. It is only important to ensure that the intended activity be carried out as it was planned or agreed, irrespective of what routes are adopted for the transfer of money and commodity. It is nothing but mere fallacy that the commodity shall pass through the ownership of finance provider to make his profit legal Islamically, *Shariah* does not offer any such magic of profit legitimacy just by possessing or owing the commodity momentarily or temporarily for some time by the financier (as argued and somehow induced in contemporary Islamic thinking). The legitimacy of profit exists in permissible economic activities even for the finance provider without any doubt and that is well justified for him too since he is contributing his money in the activity where profit is actually constructed.

What *Shariah* demands is that the commodity shall exist and the seller shall have its ownership or mandate for a valid sale, this is very pragmatic thinking on the part of *Islamic* doctrine. The ownership of commodity must go through finance provider is not a demand of *Shariah*, it's meaningless, misleading and unproductive stance. If *Shariah* demand of 'existence of commodity' is not met that will certainly make it a fraudulent sale. *Shariah* reason of 'commodity ownership or mandate' by the seller ensures that seller has the intention to sell and control of commodity in order to deliver the same to the buyer, if this condition is met once with the seller then why to repeat it through the financier in the same transaction, it makes no sense. To establish the facts of commodity existence and ownership by the seller has undeniable significance, if someone is just pretending the capability of selling the commodity without actually having the rights to sell it, is a fake offer of sale and the buyer would face the risk of not getting the delivery of the commodity, which is a deceitful situation.

These valid and established concerns of *Shariah* for the existence and control of commodity with seller or its transfer from seller to the buyer must be ensured, that can be done and protected in any suitable course taken; the truth of transference of the commodity and money shall be of prime concern that must be ensured in very commonsense. The spirit shall prevail; thus any situational terms and conditions that guarantee the enactment of truth of transfers shall be acceptable to all, pointless restrictions will only curtail the natural freedom of executing the activities.

The purpose of above reminder is to emphasize that acts and intentions must be seen in their real context, no artificial or pretending type of action be included; trade is happening between buyer and the seller only which is the fact and this truth shall be allowed to exist, the factual role of financier is to facilitate the trade by providing finance and this truth shall also be allowed to exist without introducing any make believe act.

In simplest judgment, trade is permitted in *Islamic* beliefs – so nothing can be wrong with trade provided that no prohibited commodity is the subject of trade; selling on credit is also permitted – so nothing is wrong here as well if the price on deferred payment is agreed. These are just conditions of a valid sale.

The buyer who purchases the commodity (on credit) and agrees to pay the seller at some later date, can sell the same commodity further (obviously after having the rights to sell); can sell even on credit to his buyer; or even on a lesser cash price than what he has to pay to his seller. In practice, cash selling on less than credit purchase price is frequently used by small wholesale and retail businesses, to finance their other businesses, this is trader's self financing (at cost minus) without financiers. Principally in trade, the article of trade can be priced as many times the trade happens using any cost-plus or cost-minus formula, the fixation of price is not ordained in any pragmatic philosophy including *Islamic*, and this is due to the fact that price formative factors are always changing like intrinsic value of the article of trade, its perception, circumstances, markets, supply, demand, exchange-values etc. etc.

Indisputably, selling on credit with an increase in price is permitted in *Islam*; however if seller wants to sell on cash but the buyer does not have or do not want to use his money for any reason, then this mismatch will not allow the economic activity (exchange-event) to take place, in this situation if a third body assumes the role of mediator removing the visible impediment then economic activity will happen. Now the seller sells and the mediator undertakes the function of credit. It is a very straightforward arrangement without any ill or inviting logical critique. If you remember, a criticism was cited above while discussing *Modarabah*, in case if *Mudarib* does not use his money despite having to put in; please bear in mind, that was a different situation than the case we are discussing here i.e., *Murabaha*; the difference is that *Murabaha* is a debt based financing where profit is an integral part whereas in earlier case of *Modarabah*, profit had to come through the activity, therefore these are situations nothing like each other.

In other words, the creation of debt on buyer for his own demand or choice to go in to debt was possible due to the instrumental role of mediator; on one hand, he is satisfying the requirement of buyer for the deferment of payment and simultaneously, he is also fulfilling the instant payment demand of seller. The involvement of mediator has made a fresh economic activity possible.

Now consider a previous economic activity when a credit was extended by the seller himself on a higher price than the cash price, the debt was established and the demand of buyer was initially fulfilled by the seller himself for the deferment of payment. In ever changing circumstances though, which is true for everyone, if the seller wants an immediate payment now for some valid reasons of his own, then same mediator has exactly the same role to undertake here; there is no reason why he will refuse it.

Here it comes to religious misunderstanding where such barrier is wrongly erected without any reason in the *Islamic* doctrine. Creating a debt and discounting it simultaneously is acceptable and approved by modern *Islamic* scholars that is exactly happening in permitted *Murabaha* financing but if a debt already exists then you cannot discount it. This is unbelievable and I am really unable to understand as what is the difference or where is the difference? Can we find any reason of this contradictory stance or disparity in the buyer, seller, trading activity, debt, trading subject or the financier? Actually, nothing and nowhere except for one thing i.e., the difference of debts occurrence timings. *Murabaha* financing is practically the discounting of future capital (i.e., creating debt and discounting it simultaneously).

Owing to the pretending ownership hypothesis from contemporary *Islamic* finance proponents - it is argued feebly in the defense of *Murabaha* financing that *Islamic* financier is trading thus profit is legal but this position is not accepted by any rational thinker since factually this is not the true case. Financing is not a prohibited activity rather desirable; there is no need to falsely project the financier's character as a trader; his act of facilitating the exchange-event to happen is essential and imperative and accepted logically for its economic reasons; there is no reason of rejecting his right of share or gain which is inherently justified.

•••

What exactly is the Query

In actual fact, the query is not new but as old as the inception of *Islam*, it is just re-emerged in the context of third party involvement as financier in a transaction. When *Quran* was being revealed and the prohibition of *Riba* was decreed, the nonbelievers had same subtext of query saying "Trade is like *Riba*" which was responded "Allah (SWT) has permitted the Trade and prohibited *Riba*"[10] indicating very unambiguously that Trade and *Riba* are not alike. The gist of recent query is the same as well; however the query is verbalized in several ways using different contexts that can be expressed as below.

#1 – In sale's context

Why the increase of price in a credit sale transaction of a commodity is acceptable to *Islamic* thinking while a similar increase in the principal amount of a loan is not legal when both increases are only due to the reason of delay in payment?

In other words, what are the reasons when *Islamic* sanctity is granted to an increase attached to the assets (or activity) only? Why such sanctity status cannot be assigned to the increase in money of loan, i.e., if it is not linked or associated to the assets (or activity)?

---

[10] *Quran 02:275*

#2 – In debt's perspective

If a debt is created through financing of a credit sale transaction by adding some profit to the cash price of the commodity being sold (i.e., the Cost of commodity PLUS some Profit), then how it is different from a similar debt created through a loan by adding interest to it (Principal PLUS Interest). That is – in both cases the addition is made on account for the deferment of payment akin to charging the time value of money. What makes the former debt (with built-in profit) as legitimate in *Islamic* ideology and the later unlawful?

#3 – About First Increase

Owing to the conceptual vagueness on the subject of *Riba*, some quarters of Islamic practitioners argue that an *ex-ante* increase in a loan is permissible and what in fact prohibited is increase *ex-post* (i.e., first addition of interest is permitted but not any subsequent one).

The stance further translates that impermissibility is applicable to any subsequent increase in the realization phase of profit therefore *Islamic* treatment of 'debt' and 'loan' financings shall be same initially as conventional practice is. The query from this thinking is asking why should there be any difference in the initial phase of conventional and *Islamic* handling of debts and loans. Therefore, it denounces any difference in debts created through credit sale or loan.

#4 – Of intrinsic utility

In Islamic doctrine, the money and commodities are treated differently i.e., having distinctive legal status; this division is based on the reason of intrinsic utility features. The paper money, gold and silver do not have any intrinsic value and cannot be consumed. A reason for treating the two debts differently is thus presented by many Islamic minds claiming that since money and commodity have different status hence the debt created through each is treated differently.

This argument is actually rejected by the rest of the faction on grounds that if something of intrinsic utility is used instead of paper money, gold, silver etc. (like salt, wheat, dates etc.) then the argument of 'intrinsic utility' is invalidated since debt may be created in any 'medium of exchange' that is acceptable to transacting parties. Hence, questioning minds are still unsatisfied with this reasoning and query stands without resolve as to find distinctive reasons while creating the two debts.

Summing-up the Queries

Though the two debts are resulted from two unlike debt formation processes, however since the monetary outlook of both is same hence it is almost impossible to find a difference in debts itself but only in the processes or the philosophy of debt transactions. If we try to find the reason beyond the monetary outlook of the debts than the query will actually land in a broader discipline of social science of economics. In reality, all queries are seeking answers in that sense.

In conventional money lending practices, interest is considered as an earning however the conventionalists' are failed in justifying this earning as legitimate profit as their practice of lending on interest is a function of time alone i.e., earning is based on so-called time value of money without any reference to economic activity. The arguments presented in favour of interest like the need of the society, helps the productivity, efficiency, lending operations are standardized etc. etc., are quite vague and unconvincing, firstly because the primary natural justification is not given and secondly such claims are doable without charging the interest as well. In fact, their stance is devoid of any philosophy.

At the same time there is no convincing stance from Islamic proponents except for few legal positions and feeble arguments. In effect, the matter is unresolved so far and therefore we need to look further than financial equivalences and beyond legal arguments. That is - to answer the query by establishing technical or scientific difference in two gains occurred from 'loan' and 'trade' based contracts? This exactly is the query in my view.

•••

Answering the Query

The nature is not only about biological, tangible or environmental things, but the functioning of life, the behavior of organisms, the secret phenomenon or the well-known ones and the like things; that is to say the nature covers from elementary particles to the universe in material to metaphysical description. The nature is endless and yet in every respect it seems in order and does not go out of control by itself. For the reason of such restraint found in nature, we would be justified in saying that the science of nature is very systematic and runs on principles; this belief is true for all sciences classified by the mankind i.e., the basic, applied, social sciences or subsequent branches. If any act or attempt is made to distract the systematic functioning of nature or altering or violating its set principles, eventually that will harm the nature to the degree of abuse. To become conscious for the sense and severity of any such abuse to nature, we may cite here one example of *the weapons of mass destructions* – the devastation of nature resulted by the purposeful alteration of its natural structural principles or functioning of materials e.g. of uranium.

In the context of query here, certainly the matter is related to the class of social science (the scientific study of human society and social relationships). That is – we shall study the query considering the *moral and other principles* applicable to the relationship of participants in two types of transactions. This sounds logical as well since the principles procreate the rules of law and legal understandings of affairs that in turn bring about the customs and practices (two debt creating transactions are also known practices). Therefore principally, every socially acceptable practice must have some set of rules to follow and every rule must have some principle at its origin. The question is what those principles are, moral or else, applicable to these transactions?

We may start thinking of the scientific domain first. The entire social science is the relationship of mankind with rest of the nature from environmental, biological, metaphysical to moral or else, starting from the known history of mankind, and for the sake of human species. The broader focus of social science as we value it today is **to seek the good and shun the bad** for the individuals, groups and communities, or to find the truth and curb the falsehood, to recognize the fairness and reject the wrong, or to promote the real and block the unreal, or to advocate the righteous and disapprove the evil, or to maximize the benefit and minimize the harm etc. etc. Though the evolution course of societies has made such contrasting values rather fairly evident for its meanings in mutual and communal affairs however except for few relations that are still being questioned for their **seek or shun** handling, for instance the one regarding the transactions we are trying to find an answer for.

The current economic intellect has not been able, so far, in differentiating between two transactions rather practically, is far lacking in this respect. Hence we need to explore and add some fresh thinking and moralistic reasoning to improve relevant intellect such that it may resolve the query at hand. From here onward to do so, we may revive few relevant concepts first. Then it may be suitable to depict the two debts portrayal to better comprehend and compare it. It will also be rational to discuss the modern economic intellect as how it thinks about such economic affairs. While advancing to make some intellectual progress to existing insight, you may notice dynamic thinking and reasoning challenging the present conceptual standing. A philosophical premise may not change every now and then; rather it may take decades if not centuries that a philosophical argument is challenged. The gist of query is philosophical, hence it shall be answered is similar perspective that I think is crucial and would help in understanding the answer. In effort to add some quality to the basic economics, some creative thinking is applied and tried to maintain the coherence of thoughts while introducing the fresh proposition of *economic theory of circumstances* which is though general but will answer the query logically.

Relevant Concepts

Though there are plenty of old and modern concepts that are relevant to these debt creating practices, but a few below are precisely related to the query.

Profit is Ex-Post

The Latin terms, *ex-ante* and *ex-post*, are often used in economic and monetary contexts; to refer something before the event (ex ante) and after the event (ex post). The natural law of profit is defined earlier in this book, that is - *profit is a construct of time and economic activity*, if we correlate the Latin terms with the natural law of profit then by analogy the economic activity is an event and profit is an *ex-post* reality. The relevance of Latin terms or drawing the parallel is perfect and harmonize with the stance that *profit is an ex-post fact*. It's evident by the natural law of profit that there will be no profit (no *ex-post* fact) if there is no economic activity.

It is also defined, de novo, what an economic activity is, technically explained as well and based on it a basic innovative classification scheme of economic activities is sketched out earlier in this script. There is an ideal coherence in these renovated concepts and definitions. For instance, according to the natural law of profit, a positive 'change of value' brings about profit which is an ex-post fact. Likewise, profit can be predetermined in activities like trade when the realized profit equals estimated profit. However, profit cannot be enforced until the economic activity is not concluded with the presence of profit. The attribute of *'predetermined'* only implies that the cost of economic process in few classes of economic activities (like trade) is either known or non-existent therefore the realized profit is same as that was estimated. On the other hand, if the process of economic activity is such that the determination of its cost is not possible like in several productions then the profit will be undetermined. Thus the determination or indetermination of *profit* is a matter dependent on the knowledge of the cost of economic process employed in economic activity, if this cost is known – the profit may be predetermined, and if not estimable then the profit is undetermined. Yet, this judgment of cost does not and cannot change the ex-post reality of profit which is only enforceable on the conclusion of economic activity and the availability of profit as a result. In short and in principle, the profit can be ex-post-predetermined or ex-post-undetermined.

Interest is Ex-Ante

We have demonstrated earlier that the conventional lending does not comply with the natural law of profit, and neither any other human law nor philosophy is in notice that may bear with their lending practices. In a conventional loan arrangement – Interest is enforced simultaneously when the lending contract is activated regardless of any concern to the use of lent money or the economic activity if there is any; therefore Interest is an ex-ante-predetermined element. Lending is the event by analogy and Interest is the ex-ante element. The enforcement of Interest shall mean the fixation of liability for making the payment at some later date.

If the debtor does not pay on due date and contract is revived, renewed or rewritten to resettle his liability on a further due date then technically the transaction will not be considered as closed since only the agreed time period is lapsed but other terms are not fulfilled. If previous terms of Interest are upheld or a change in Interest amount or Interest rate is also re-negotiated at this stage – even then the Interest will only be seen as an ex-ante-predetermined reality. The resettlement or reinstatement of Interest with extension in time period will remain an ax-ante reality of lending event and will be seen as a continuation of previously agreed contract. From first to all subsequent Interest manifestations in a lending contract are enforced up-front thus ex-ante. Hence, Interest (ex-ante-predetermined) element in a loan or lending transaction cannot be equated to Profit (ex-post-predetermined) of a trade transaction. Thus, Profit and Interest are technically different, that we can say before any economic argument of differentiation.

Exchange-Value Specifics

The puzzle of 'value' in economics is perhaps more complex and disputed matter than the subject of *Riba*. If we move on from philosophical debate on value to its practical manifestation, then applying 'exchange-value' concept instead of 'value' may help us resolve several unresolved issues. It is thus appropriate here to list few specific and inherent features that are well-known and undisputed for the meanings of 'exchange-value':

1. All commodities (articles of trade) may have a relative exchange-value to each other at any given time.

2. Price of any article of trade is the exchange-value of the same denoted in any medium of exchange like money.

3. Every exchange-value has a life either defined by the nature, by perception associated to it, or set by negotiation when exchanged. This is true for all articles of trade whatsoever.

4. Several exchange-value lives are possible for an article of trade, this life count depends on how many times the article is traded.

5. A change in the exchange-value of an article can occur without any qualitative or intrinsic change within the article of trade itself.

6. Every *economic output* has a life too, during this life - it may have as many exchange-value lives as the nature allows or it goes through the process of negotiations for exchange.

7. The use or utility of an *economic output* might cause a decrease in its intrinsic value thus the exchange-value, this reduction in value may be recognized as the transference of value

from *exchange-value* to *impact-value* (not use value), e.g., use of an automobile.

8. The **profit** once incorporated in an exchange-value of a commodity or product becomes an integral part of the exchange-value (and so the price); a positive change of value (profit) by definition endorses the act as an economic activity. Similarly, in case of loss, a change of value occurs but with converse tendency.

9. The **money** has a fixed exchange-value that is assigned to it as a rule without exception, the Interest charged on money does not become an integral part of the money since it cannot increase the assigned or face value of money; therefore Interest is always treated separately for all accounting purposes.

The Two Debts Portrayal

As we know, the two debt transactions are exchange of different exchange-values involving time, thus above *exchange-value specifics* are directly related to the query and will remain in the backdrop while comparing the two debts portrayal; the two debts which are identical in financial outlook but created through unlike courses of trading and lending; the two practices are already perceived as distinct deeds. Let's consider a practically possible scenario of two debts (by example) as below:

In this example, all trade transactions are executed by creating debt with built-in profit i.e., a manufacturer of cars sells a car to its exporter who further exports it to its distributor in another country; the distributor vends out the car to his reseller; the reseller retails the car either to his customer (user) or through a bank to bank's customer. The first customer utilizes it for some time and then sells out to some other user, and so on. Let us assume that from manufacturer to current user of car, there were twenty trade transactions executed in total (perhaps twenty exchange-value lives as well if the car was traded at different price each time).

If we correlate above trading scenario to our creative classification scheme of economic activities, then from manufacturer to the first user of car, all trade activities are possibly of augmentation type (positive change to occur in the exchange-value of the car) as expected that every business entity would add some profit in its sale price; while from first user to the current user of car, all trade activities are of diminution type as expected from them to discount by taking out the impact value at sale.

To compare the debts created in trade, we will create an identical transactions pattern of loan based debts; let's assume - twenty lending transactions are executed at the same time in parallel with each trade happening. The Interest charged is exactly the same as the built-in profit or loss of trade based debt. Following initial values are used to populate the two debts in next table:

Table 9 : Example - Input Values

Debt Details	Figures
Manufacturer's Credit Price or Trade Debt =	100,000
Manufacturer's built-in profit (@10%) =	9,091
Lender's Principal Amount Lent =	90,909
Interest charged (@10%) on Loan amount =	9,091
The Debt created through lending =	100,000

Since the profit or loss becomes integral part of the exchange-value of traded article (car) therefore no split accounting of profit or loss is required; however as the Interest cannot become an integral part of the money lent thus treated alone, a separate column is created in the table to register the Interest, this column is labeled as 'Extra Liability' on table header.

The first liability created in two debts is the same; let us apply the same rate of profit or loss and the Interest (i.e., 10%) to all successive transactions to maintain the table simple and clear. One can clearly see that all trade and loan based debts are the same; profit and Interest entries are also the same exactly i.e., identical financial outlook of the two debts, except one unusual column (i.e., of Extra Liability), the rest columns are usual.

Table 10 : Example – Two Debts Scenario

EVL	Debt from Trade			Debt from Lending			Extra Liability
	Price	Debt	Profit	Principal	Interest	Debt	
1	100,000	100,000	9,091	90,909	9,091	100,000	9,091
2	110,000	110,000	10,000	100,000	10,000	110,000	19,091
3	121,000	121,000	11,000	110,000	11,000	121,000	30,091
4	133,100	133,100	12,100	121,000	12,100	133,100	42,191
5	146,410	146,410	13,310	133,100	13,310	146,410	55,501
6	133,100	133,100	12,100	121,000	12,100	133,100	67,601
7	121,000	121,000	11,000	110,000	11,000	121,000	78,601
8	110,000	110,000	10,000	100,000	10,000	110,000	88,601
9	100,000	100,000	9,091	90,909	9,091	100,000	97,692
10	90,909	90,909	8,264	82,645	8,264	90,909	105,956
11	82,645	82,645	7,513	75,131	7,513	82,645	113,469
12	75,131	75,131	6,830	68,301	6,830	75,131	120,300
13	68,301	68,301	6,209	62,092	6,209	68,301	126,509
14	62,092	62,092	5,645	56,447	5,645	62,092	132,154
15	56,447	56,447	5,132	51,316	5,132	56,447	137,285
16	51,316	51,316	4,665	46,651	4,665	51,316	141,950
17	46,651	46,651	4,241	42,410	4,241	46,651	146,191
18	42,410	42,410	3,855	38,554	3,855	42,410	150,047
19	38,554	38,554	3,505	35,049	3,505	38,554	153,552
20	35,049	35,049	3,186	31,863	3,186	35,049	156,738

EVL represents corresponding exchange-value-life number of the car, whereas Price and Profit, Principal and Interest, two debts columns represent respective subjects we are familiar with; the new column of extra liability is the sum of all interest charged, this will be explained subsequently. The graphic form of above is:

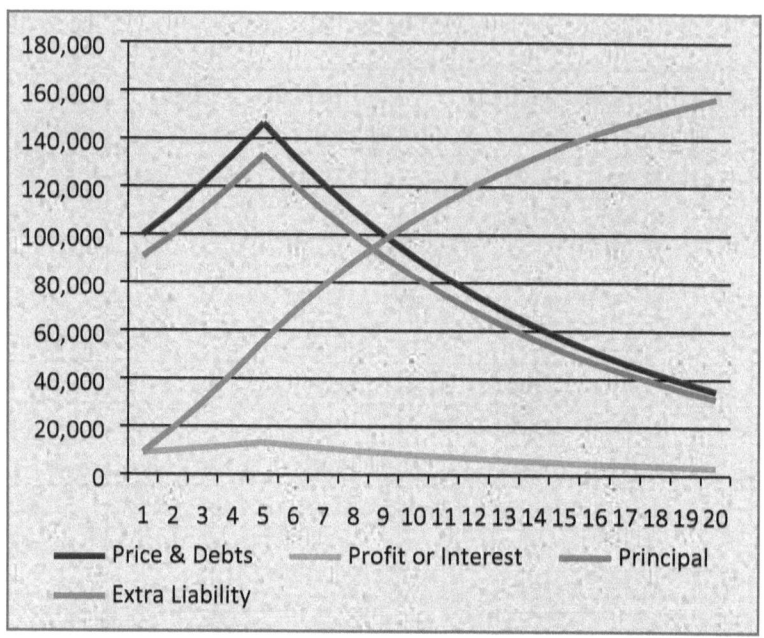

Figure 13 : Debts Picture & Extra Liability

There is no surprise in this plot except the red trace. We already knew this similarity i.e., the price and two debts are identical, profit and Interest are the same and if we add the Interest curve to the principal curve, the resultant curve is the debt curve. Only the red trace labeled as the 'extra liability' is drawing our attention to look into it thoroughly since it is unusual and might be holding any point of differentiation we are looking for, this may have economic character. The significancy of 'extra liability' will be discussed in the last section of this chapter while elaborating the answer to the query.

Modern Economic Intellect

If economics is a science of people and society then its prime idea shall revolve around offering justice to them individually as well as collectively; societal justice is premeditated (framed up, laid-out) in customs and norms primarily that survive as a result of civilization struggle of the people and societies or available in given divine doctrines; respecting standards is binding on all. Principally, if an alteration is to be made in any social norm or standard (developed by humans; no change in divine stuff is agreeable), than the modified form of the standard shall offer the same shared justice in addition to communal approval. In this perspective, we may look in to the case of 'lending on Interest' in its societal perspective before economic comparison of the two.

Societal Norms – Right or Wrong?

We all live with our particular natures, tendencies, limitations and circumstances; every individual has its own thinking and abilities, propensity to consume and to produce, to decide among preferences while always seeking freedom of choices etc. For instance in regard to the freedom of choices available to me to fulfill my desire of taking tea, I may spend just two rupees for a cup of tea at a road-side truck drivers' hotel (chappar hotel) on my way back to home or may spend more than hundred rupees for similar quantity cup of tea at a five-star hotel located just on the other side of the road; from these choices accessible to me, my decision to go to the expensive five-star hotel, as I believe, is sensible and economical for me since I know myself, I am quite sensitive to hygienic conditions and for me opting to an inexpensive two rupee cup of tea may eventually cost me five times more (than apparently expensive choice) when I pay the physician's fee for the treatment of my stomach disorder caused by unhygienic conditions of the chappar hotel. The point is – a seemingly expensive choice is not expensive for me in fact; the finance and economics are at least different by that degree in the first place.

The people roaming around the same place of hotels may choose one of the two, everyone would have its own seminal reason to decide among choices available for the desire of taking tea, and collectively there could be a multiplicity of reasons for the two choices.

Similarly, even though one may have cash in hand to purchase a car on spot settlement, however he may opt to buy the same on credit terms for his own reasons including that of very economic nature. If a costly cup of tea was economical for me, then there may be same or similar reason for him to purchase the car on future payment basis - to be in debt is one's own choice, what price has to do here? The price sum he will eventually pay in installments by including an agent in between will definitely be much more than the price option he had for cash payment; his decision of purchasing via debt route is beneficial to him in his economic sense. If he were able to approach the manufacturer directly to purchase the car and the manufacturer had a policy to retail on credit, certainly then he had to pay much less than what he is paying now to the reseller or the bank, so the price (exchange-value against money) is just a choice available or choice-in-access for the intended purchase on buyers' preferred terms.

Surely, I am not wrestling with any theory of value here, but emphasizing just on following touchstones:

1. We are the best judge of our own affairs and concerns, economic in nature or else, after the Almighty Creator.

2. The freedom of choice is everyone's basic and undeniable right limited only by accessibility.

Since the beginning of human interactions, people are trained, accustomed and cultured to acquire other's property by negotiation in exchange of what they can offer and acceptable to their counterparts. However the negotiation of counter-values for a fair equivalence that can be acceptable on both sides of exchange had always been a difficult task because of inherent complexity in the concept of value. Whereas, it looks indecisive how value could be defined, then whoever logician gave the idea of the medium of exchange or money, in fact did a great favour to the humanity, because it gives decisive autonomy to persons or property owners to symbolize their work, property, and intellect as they find suitable in their circumstances with knowledge and experience they possess to do so; while additionally the society works on standards in this way.

If five-star hotel had set a price of hundred rupee for its cup of tea, the hotel attendant will not accept if I pay rupees two after having the tea, rather he might thump me on my nose or penalize me some other way. He will be justified in his actions and other people around will also support his stance since I was trying to violate the known informal agreement or general understanding. The point here is that though one is free to choose an option available to him but that must be in agreement with the counterpart in a mutual kind of affair.

Although, we all are the part of the society, but with all our personal privileges and social relationships, we don't get the right in our individual or social capacities to alter the norms of society that it had established for the functioning of the community. If the society had devised a medium of exchange (*that might be anything either a piece of paper, gold, silver or any other metal or material article, the suitability of this medium's material or its properties are not in question here*) as a social contract to serve the community and to be used by the people for mutual or group exchanges of values, then whoever try to contravene that norm - will upset the interactions of people and thus effect the society badly. If money as a medium of exchange, is used to price the values to set the exchange-value of people's commodities, products, or services, then how it would not upset the interaction of people in a society when money itself is priced? The lending of money on Interest (i.e. pricing money) is a clear violation of societal norms; no differing view is justified since no such rationalization is ever identified.

There is no rational answer or justification ever presented from the proponents of lending on Interest practices, the points to emphasize here are:

1. All interactions of exchangeable-values in a society are mutual or social contracts among interacting parties having participants' respective benefits contained within.

2. It's binding and obligatory on all to respect societal norms like money or any 'medium of exchange'; any violation is inexcusable and unjustifiable.

Let me reiterate on the matter of *value* in context of what is said above, there are millions of products and billions of people around; each product has a relative exchange-value to the other, changing invariably with time; every individual is a case of distinct disposition, owing its persistently varying circumstances; this is what the nature is – unimaginable and indescribable.

That is why I think – no agreement on the issue - "what is value" is reached and neither seems possible so I guess. Ultimately, the only method left for people to exchange their produce is by self or market fixing of the value as exchange-value by using medium of exchange standards for handling so complex dynamics and realm of the nature and value. How people can survive (live peacefully) and interact (justifiably) without respecting each other and complying with societal principles?

Money cannot be priced since it is a social yardstick to measure or price exchange-values i.e., to quantify or understand the vague value. This is exactly the same as to quantify the length, breadth, distance etc. we make use of inch, foot, meter, mile or else standards. I cannot make my own length measuring yardstick of 38 inches or more and ask the cloth merchant to measure cloth using my yardstick, or even the merchant cannot make his own and use it, because standards are the constant frameworks of specifications. Having said that and without any rational argument against this stance in my knowledge, what surprises me the most is - asking the reason again and again for outlawing the 'lending on Interest (pricing the money)' in the divine doctrines. Is the violation of societal norms alone is not enough for the prohibition? Do the conventional economists have built any justified financial economics resting on this bare contempt? Is economics some supra-natural science that may cure the harm, supernaturally, caused by abusing the social norms? Results are evident, the concepts of right and wrong are buried, just benefit has become the prime motive of people no matter how one assures it; the rationality from the society is vanishing.

Economic Rationale of Differentiation

The contextual and inferential meanings of 'value' and 'exchange-value' are nothing like each other; value is seen in idiosyncratic (individualistic) context such as perception and utility, while the gist of exchange-value is necessarily seen in mutual or communal perspective based on aspects like shared vision, market and market conditions. An individual (person or business) with its current economic status is always a potential and ready economic agent. Then the exchange which brings the individual's economy in contact with societal economy, acquires the status of a special event since the former (individual's economy) which itself is a factor of the later, stimulates and regenerates the societal economy (the anthology of individual economies). This cyclic occurrences based on *exchange events* has two dynamic features of economic enormity, one toward individual's economy and the other towards the shared economy, thus having a pivotal place in creating an equilibrium between two economies; any anomaly between start and finishing point of the event with an immediate or subsequent effect in any one direction will eventually effect the second since the two are interrelated. The state of economic equilibrium here is imperative.

Though the modern thinking of 'economic balance or equilibrium' is derived from the equilibrium defined in physical science; however this is an imperfect way of correlating two distinct classes of science i.e., basic and social; the reason is – the basic sciences revolve around materials and based on materialistic evidences whereas social sciences revolve around the person and based on moralistic reasoning. This imperfect correlation is thus translated in to an imperfect hypothesis of adapting the 'physical forces' concept to 'economic forces'.

The age old demand and supply philosophies make a lot of sense for the subjects of price and supplies, but theorizing economic equilibrium as the equivalence of demand and supply in modern thinking is a distasteful idea. It is basically contradicting to the basic premise of the social science that encircles the people, society and relationship between them as a whole. The *demand* of anything (for its price and supply conditions) is always based on purchasing power of a partial segment of the society. Therefore economic equilibrium, in its current understanding, has a limited relevance to that part of society and may not be regarded as a social sciences' thinking. However, since current economic equilibrium idea is only for those who are producing and those who are consuming some specific produce, therefore it may be recognized as managerial level subject of business only but not as any social science hypothesis related to people and society in general.

The imitated idea of equilibrium from physics has actually shaped the study of economics more like a part of material sciences rather than a true social science study and as a result has shifted the focus of economics away from the populace effectively. Anyway, we cannot indulge in such a debate of differing fundamentals. We will find the conditions of equilibrium merely coherent in our way of economic thinking and are more relevant to the people and society practically, that is – the states or conditions of equilibrium in an 'exchange event'.

The Reality of Exchange-Event

In view of our fresh definition of economic activity, the objects of worth can be transferred in unilateral or bilateral ways. The unilateral transfers include charity, gifts, inheritances or else forms of allocating resources to economic entities etc., however the bilateral transfer has just one form i.e., the exchange-event. If truth be told, most of unilateral transfers are actually possible because of previously concluded bilateral transfers. In that context, the bilateral transfers or exchange-events are the exclusive economic events.

The exchange-event, which is the whole and sole life of an economy – for all economies; which is the raison d'être in the formation and existence of economy, shall be the primary investigative subject (in my view) for all sorts of fundamental economic issues like the one we have at hand.

The building of an economy is a never-ending and exigent task. Essentially, every economy is built using the bricks of exchange-events, brick by brick, having no exception whatsoever. If no exchange-event is taking place, will mean there is no building of economy; if the quantum of exchange-events is decreasing or the sum is not meeting optimum level, it will mean the economy is not progressing but crumbling etc. Technically, every exchange-event has a natural velocity of its execution defined by the circumstances of the participants and actual dynamics of economic process; any reason that accelerates or decelerates the velocity is not beneficial for the wellbeing of any economy. A rational well doing architect of economy will always look for quality bricks (beneficial exchange-events) and will ensure the timely setting up of the same to make and keep the economy in good health. In brief, exchange-event is pivotal to the building and the quality of an economy.

Since exchange-event is the primary subject in our economic thinking, therefore we may recognize specific aspects understood or related to its economic concept.

1. *Exchange* is a function while *exchange-event* is an incident testifying the happening of the function.

2. An *exchange-event* is a formal or informal deal, of giving and receiving, similar or unlike things of some worth or economic significance, including goods, services or else exchangeable values.

3. An *exchange* might be planned to happen at some time in the future; or to materialize in parts over a period of time; however it will be recognized as an *exchange-event* when it actually had happened with completion.

4. The completion of an *exchange-event* shall mean that the delivery of exchangeable things has been concluded by respective participants of the event to their counterparts as agreed mutually.

5. There are *pre* and *post exchange-event* subjects of study that are linked to or can be seen in context of the *exchange-event* under question.

6. One significant *pre-exchange-event* subject is the capacity of the participants to fulfill the promise of delivery at agreed terms and conditions.

7. One significant *post-exchange-event* subject is the satisfaction of the participants from the event in view of their expectations and possibilities.

The Cause of Exchange-Event

Given that every economic agent is the best judge of its own affairs and actions, thus it shall not be eccentric to say that the **basic cause of an exchange event exists in the circumstances of the participants**; the circumstances of economic agents may be defined as the anthology of economic variables and natural tendencies in current state as offered by them at the start of exchange event. This will also sound a fundamentally differing thought vis-à-vis current economic thinking and will also attach 'circumstances' of economic agents as the focal subject of exchange in place of 'value' and 'counter-value'. The change of idiosyncratic 'value' to 'circumstances' has its verifiable basis in *Shariah* as well, having said that, it is however not possible for me to include here or further elaborate on the subject due to its vastness that would perhaps need another book volume of work.

The 'circumstances' of a person is the most relevant idea in context of the social science subject; if endorsed by social scientists as the true cause of 'exchange event' in every occurrence then we may agree at some point of distinction between the two debts and gains. I tried to speculate over and over again with a critical eye while exploring why one will not endorse this idea but didn't find any reason that someone will reject it by realizing its social and economic sense. It has rather encouraged me to present here an original economic theory of mine based on this causal idea of 'circumstances' as the basic cause of an *exchange-event* that takes place in each and every instance. As a consequence of adapting the cause, other subjects of study in this discipline like economic equilibrium or economic justice would also be seen in the context of the circumstances of economic agents.

Economic Theory of Circumstances (ETC)

Economics is a branch of social science - the study of human society and social relationships; by definition of social science per se, the discipline of economics must actually deliberate entirely on the person only because society is the union of persons and social relationships are also formed between persons even if relations are created through businesses. The reality of a person for the science of economics (as distinctive subject) is not its biology (body) rather the life and living of the body as an aware creature. Everybody is in a particular state of life and living conditions at a given point in time that may collectively be referred to as the circumstances of the body (economic agent) at that moment which tends to change, now and then, as a rule of life. The varying feature of circumstances, intermittently, is true for any or every person or business entity. Hence logically, the present or foreseeable 'state of circumstances' of any economic entity (person or business) may only be one of three possibilities i.e., either it is declining, stagnant or progressing at a given point in time.

The fact of the 'state of circumstances' is best known to the economic entity alone, however external entities may have a conjectural view on the fact. One universal fact is though known to everyone that the humans and active businesses are nonstop consuming machines, and this ceaseless feature has a tendency of pulling the current economic status of the entity to a backward state. Logically therefore, every economic entity, in its rational state of mind will always be acting in one of the two intentional modes i.e., either to prevent it from worsening off its current circumstances, or to become better-off as compared to its current status; there is no third attitude expected from a practical and sensible economic entity for its economic actions.

Basic Theorems of ETC

Owing to this preliminary view, we have two basic and pivotal theorems from ETC as below:

> *The present or foreseeable 'state of circumstances' of any economic entity (person or business) may only be one of the three possibilities i.e., either it is declining, stagnant or progressing at a given point in time.*

> *Every economic entity, in its rational state of mind will always be acting in one of the two intentional modes i.e., either to prevent it from worsening off its current circumstances, or to become better-off as compared to its current status; there is no third attitude expected from a practical and sensible economic entity for its economic actions.*

The two intentional modes of actions by economic entity (i.e., preventing worse-off, becoming better-off) though may have several activities within each state of circumstances (i.e., declining, stagnant, progressing), however to become better-off is an attitude essentially rooted in gainful economic activities (like creation and augmentation classes in our original scheme); whereas, economic entity's acts for preventing it from going to a worse-off state are certainly based on sustaining type of economic activities.

The science which revolves around the person of so complex diversities may look simple but in actuality is more complex than basic sciences. The man, its nature and its circumstances are so intertwined together that any partial or isolated thinking about this trilogy may never be a convincing attempt. In reality, the triune for its economic behavior is very broad. In view of the fact that human being are dignified creature having various other motivations to act than merely working for gains in monetary terms; they act to help others, to please or be grateful to fellow humans or the almighty Creator, to achieve spiritual satisfaction and to do something for becoming better-off in the hereafter (i.e., the economic activity is being carried out on earth and expected gain is constructed in the heavens) etc. Therefore gainful and better-off philosophy of person includes all human sensitivities beside its monetary import. Unfortunately, economics has become a political and financial subject in real life, to a great extent, for the reason of downing the dignified character of the person. However, in our thinking, all aspects of human nature are integrated in 'economic theory of circumstances' for total economic behavior of man directed towards an exchange-event in practical life. This is another basic premise of ETC.

Referring to the two theorems derived earlier, the underside of the theory of circumstances is built on two realms of tendencies held by an economic entity i.e., *the mode of its actions* and *the state of its circumstances*; two number of modes and three number of states will set a statistic of total possible economic relations when two economic entities are engaged in an exchange-event. Obviously, each shall be in either of the two modes (in order to simplify referring to these modes subsequently let us symbolize - the mode of preventing worse-off as PWO and becoming better-off as BBO). There we may have a maximum of three possible situations once they meet up for an economic interaction i.e., the probable situations of exchange-event in view of modes, are:

1) Both are in PWO mode

2) One in PWO mode, and other in BBO

3) Both are in BBO mode

Let us first characterize the two modes of PWO and BBO as understood or implied within ETC and then we may discuss the three situations one by one.

If you hark back to earlier arguments on the natural law of profit, it was construed that the profit for the one is to come from the counterpart economic entity in an exchange-event. You may also recall that all economic entities are non-stop consuming machines; therefore it may further imply that these value burning engines will certainly have some specific consumption levels as well to live or sustain. So the two facts that the profit has to come from the counterpart in an exchange-event and the economic entities will have certain consumption level to live or sustain, are the defining truths to realize and characterize the modes i.e., PWO and BBO.

Thus PWO – *preventing worse-off mode*; implies that the economic entity is striving to maintain its current level of consumption and has little or nothing to offer to his counterpart as profit; it also implies that any gain for him from an exchange for his survival is not a profit as long as he remains in this mode; a loss or no gain will further worsen his status.

Next BBO – *becoming better-off mode*; implies that the economic entity carrying this mode has enough at its disposal to meet its current level of consumption and is also able to offer some profit from his stores to the counterpart economic entity in exchange of some profitable gain in his favour. It also implies that a profit will further elevate its economic status however certain specific level of losses may change his mode to PWO status.

The two modes are not permanent features attached to economic entities, rather PWO entity can turn into BBO and the vice versa. One or many exchange-events shall be instrumental in modifying the current status of an economic entity from PWO to BBO or the vice versa; whereas profit or loss are perhaps the most significant expected reasons for these occurrences of change.

We may now discuss the exchange-event situations.

Situation #1: Both are in PWO mode

Both are intentionally preventing itself from going in to the worse-off or further worse-off state. It means none of them is in a position to offer any gain or profit to his counterpart without exposing itself to sacrifice. A gain can be anything but *profit to his counterpart* shall always mean a gain which is more than consumption level of the counterpart. If an economic entity agrees to sacrifice for any reason to offer a gain or profit to his counterpart, that may cause further worsening off its current circumstances. Naturally thus, both entities will not desire to undergo an exchange at deterioration; there is no probability of exchange-event to take place with profit to anyone. Only a sacrifice by one in favour of the other can make the exchange-event to happen.

If any exchange-event do happen between them - it will only be for the reason of supporting or maintaining the current state of circumstances (or to meet current level of consumption) of one or both economic entities without any profit to anyone (e.g., perceptive exchange under transference category in our novel classification scheme); the motive behind such exchange-event may be of some humane kind, a 'mutual cooperative' type of transaction or the like. This is important to register, if anyone of them tries to inflict some profit in his favour then he must not be carrying the PWO mode and the next situation shall apply in such a case.

Situation #2: One in PWO mode, and other in BBO

The two economic bodies are carrying unlike modes of actions here; the one in mode PWO as portrayed just above, will not be in a position to grant any profit to the other unless he is not further deprived of his current economic state. We may not forget that PWO entity is a consuming engine too and need to live and sustain; it's impossible to ignore the intake feature of the entity and therefore his need is irrefutable. The gravity of his need to sustain may force him to accept and compromise his long term further worsening off his circumstances to his short term sustaining pressure. This tendency of economic body if repeated will form a perpetual loop of exchange-events for now sustaining bargain at the cost of additional worse-off effects in the future and will eventually kill this body economically at point when he would have nothing to sacrifice.

On the other hand, the other economic body bearing BBO mode (i.e., to become better-off or further better-off and thus seeking profit) will have few options while he meets up the body in PWO mode, for instance:

a) BBO by recognizing the state of circumstances of his counterpart can refuse to interact with him for the reason of not having a genuine prospect of profit in such exchange-event.

b) BBO may also insist on immediate profit from PWO without considering or knowing the economic circumstances of the body in PWO mode.

c) BBO can compromise to postpone his objective of profit for now until the other body moves on to the better-off mode when a profit can actually be constructed or if constructed.

d) BBO can help the other PWO economic body to sustain, within his own capacity of doing so that does not bring him in the worse-off mode; BBO being in the state of progress shall always have this cooperative capacity, extending cooperation is common human instinct, businesses are also run by human beings. Every kind of economic cooperation with or without monetary gain is good for the societal economy.

Rationally, PWO-BBO interaction is a 'not for profit' state of affairs, no profit is existing without depriving the economic body in PWO mode; in this situation as well, a justifiable economic activity shall only be that of sustaining type; any profit is unwarranted here though achievable only by force, compulsion or exploitation. Let us brood over again, only BBO is seeking profit but his counterpart is not, and neither PWO can offer any profit without sacrificing on his part therefore there is no fair and socially defensible profit for BBO at the cost of further worsening-off of PWO economic entity.

By virtue of the **golden rule** (*i.e., think, do and feel for others as you think, do and feel for yourself*) demanding good and fair play for everyone by everyone, the society will not approve a gain at the cost of an economic body going worse-off. It was previously pointed out what a sustaining type of activity is, yet it is good to reiterate the difference between a profitable and sustaining type of activity just to ensure the intended sense of the two. In this outlook, all economic activities improving the current circumstances of the economic body are to be entitled as profitable or gainful, and all activities that help economic bodies to maintain their current level of circumstances but do not improve in economic sense shall be regarded as sustaining type of activities. It'll be an oversight if any sustaining activity is considered as profitable (gainful) just because of the compensation that prevents this PWO economic body from further worsening-off his circumstances. This is an important consideration to avoid any muddling up.

Situation #3: Both are in BBO mode

Normally, most of economic entities in an economy are in BBO mode; if not in majority then the status of nation ought to be panicky or unsettled; the prosperity level of an economy may perhaps be measured if this figure or statistics is known. When such entities meet up (i.e., both are in BBO mode), obviously the profit on both sides is the motive in the intended exchange. The meet up also implies that they are ready to offer some gain or profit from their stores to their counterpart, expecting in exchange to receive some gain or profit from him as well. This readiness attitude of economic bodies will only need them to negotiate and agree on the terms and conditions for the transference of the objects that each of them is or will be possessing, and when they do agree – the exchange event might occur instantly or in an agreed time frame. If exchange-event is instant (like buy or sell by cash), their respective gains will be achieved straight away; however if the exchange-event needs some time period to conclude, then one or both economic bodies may have to wait for their respective gains until the event ends.

Other than the spiritual gain, all gains are visible by effect or being tangible, and without any exception, all the gains are transferred from one entity to the other by means of the objects exchanged between them (*it's a natural and constant rule for material or worldly gain that every gain has a carrier in the form of an object*). In view of that, the two interacting BBO economic bodies will have their respective gains in object(s) that they receive from each other.

Principally, there might be as many unique gains as the number of objects exist in exchange-event. If there is just one object involved, then there will be just one gain that shall be shared or divided between them since both are in BBO mode, if the single gain in sum goes to any one entity only, then the situation of interaction will not be considered as BBO-BBO but BBO-PWO.

So far, we have discussed three situations based on two modes of actions only without going further deep into the internal state of circumstances of interacting bodies. Logically, the PWO economic body will have its internal current state either stagnant or declining. The BBO economic body will be having its current internal state of circumstances as stagnant or progressing. The internal state of circumstances will make a decision for the mode of action of a rational economic body.

One may have several questions with regards to the modes of actions and internal state of economic bodies, such as – why every economic entity is not in the same BBO mode as logically everyone would like to become better-off? The internal state of 'stagnant' is common to both types of economic bodies, how common in two unlike modes? Such and other such questions might be answered if some further clarification is offered on ETC concept; few thinking tips may also help to realize why ETC enfolds larger social science under the discipline of economics than the economics defined today.

Suppose, you are located in an economy where you have no opportunity in your access to jump from your current declining state of circumstances to a better-off situation; or in a contrary sense – such opportunity is available but you are not in a position or not capable to benefit from the same even if you wish to change your status; in both cases and despite your will – you can't change your current declining state of circumstances to the better-off condition. So, it is not a matter of 'liking' or 'willing' to define your mode of action or mind-set but your circumstances are the decisive factor to define your rational intent and possible mode of action. If it is not possible for you to move to a position that you like and your current state is declining then what shall you do rationally – to prevent yourself from going further worse-off. It will not be a rational attitude but wishful if your economic condition is declining and you cannot move to a better-off position because of circumstances but still you keep eye on something which is not in your access or capability. This attitude cannot be accepted as rational since you cannot create a connection between your target and current status. Though it may also not be possible for you to prevent yourself from further worsening off your circumstances, however when you are a rational living economic entity and for the reason being a consuming machine too – you have no other option but to strive for living and prevent yourself from going into a further deteriorated state.

If the private or internal state of circumstances of an economic entity is 'stagnant', that shall mean - he is in an economic loop providing him the vital sustainable consuming supplies. Then if he can offer profit to his counterpart in an exchange-event, he shall be carrying BBO mode but if he can't offer then obviously his mode of action will be regarded as PWO.

ETC may redefine economics

In my view the current academic definition given to the discipline of economics (*i.e., the social science that studies the production, distribution, and consumption of goods and services*) encircles a very niche and reduced spectrum of the social science than what it should have been by the very definition of social science per se (*i.e., the academic disciplines associated with the society and the relationships amongst individuals within a society*). If an individual, not involved in the production, distribution or consumption of goods and services, where is he in economics by the very definition of social science? Will it imply that economics is not a social science subject then? Or, the poor person is not a part of society? The reason of leaving such an individual out of the purview of the discipline of economics renders its definition as seriously deficient; economics must be redefined thus.

It looks that the current definition of economics is not envisioned by any philosophical minds but by some legal or professional minds since it leaves out so much of a person for its economic character that could have never been ignored by a philosophical mind. Perhaps, the narrow definition serves the political and financial power manipulators, enjoying space in confusion. The politically and financially entrenched western world may not give a thought to new economic paradigm but the Islamic world can accept a thinking shift since it is seeking a different system than the conventional one.

The Economics in ETC

The present imprecise definition of economics is not coherent with its original class of social science; there is little economics in the discipline of economics by the very definition of social science. While, the distinctive paradigm of ETC encircles full and complete spectrum of economics under the ambit of social science; we may give good reasons for this claim of ETC integrity using few corresponding logical facts and justifiable beliefs, within defining and comparing statements as phrased in following points.

1. As for the definition - economy is a state of few economic variables of an economic jurisdiction (*from individual economic entity to the world*).

2. Every individual (person or business) in itself is an economic jurisdiction thus has its own realm of economy; whereas the societal economy is the anthology of individual economies of that society and that is an undeniable logical reality.

3. Thus when each individual economy is a factor of societal economy, then it must be in relationship to other individual economies.

4. The relationship is a state of being connected, no matter if being in an active or inactive state with other individual economies or society.

5. Every individual economy (person or business) is always active as long as it is alive; this is different vis-à-vis active or inactive state of relationship.

6. Economics is a branch of social science, whereas the social science is related to the society and the relationships amongst individuals in a society.

7. Hence, every existing individual economic entity (person or business) is a part of economy; no one is left out by the very definition of social science.

8. Thus, the social science of economics is the study of individuals (person or business) and society; for their exclusive current state of circumstances, economic actions and plans together with results of the same on individuals and society.

9. Contrarily, the current definition of economics will recognize only active individuals (person or business) involved in production, distribution or consumption activities leaving all other activities and inactive individuals out of its sphere.

Other than covering the full domain of economics as expected for it being a branch of the social science, ETC has an altogether different idea while looking towards the working of economic affairs. The philosophy here is poles apart to what we see in conventional economics, however no philosophical comparison is offered here since the book is not on the subject of economics rather it shall only include the relevant part to our context of query. Accordingly, philosophical postulates of ETC are presented here for the purpose on hand.

The Relevant Philosophy of ETC

In my view, any humane, rational, ethical or Islamic economics shall take following factors as basic building blocks of philosophy for the study of this discipline and subsequent professional work and implementation:

1. The *cause of an economic action* by an individual (person or business) has its reason in its current 'state of circumstances'.

2. The basic *cause of an exchange-event* also has its reason in the circumstances of the participants.

3. The economic behaviors of participants (or the mode of actions) are defined by the state of their circumstances at the time of exchange-event.

4. The exchange-event is the basic building block of an economy and instrumental in the transfer of

wealth or value (with or without any gain or loss) from one economic entity to the other.

5. The motives of participants in an exchange-event are achieved only through the objects exchanged between them in corresponding incidents.

6. The exchange-event is the exclusive affair where economic justice can be built to the participants and if not done then nowhere else it can be done by any subsequent method.

The *value* is not a permanent feature of any object or service and neither it can ever be, for the simple reason that everything around is changing invariably. Simply, you can't offer any statement defining *what the value is* actually. Objectively, it is possible that any produce has some intrinsic value and some labour value is also put in to it making it an exchangeable produce that is seen and desired by someone subjectively at one instance or in one case but not at another instance or in another case. So what is the *value* of that produce if you want to relate to the produce, there is no answer? The "paradox of value" and other confusions related to the subject of value in western economics have at least one reason of distraction common to all the objective and subjective theories of *value* and that is – theorists see the *value* in an individualistic context of an object or the individual. Objectively, *value* is neither a permanent feature nor your subjective judgment for the worth of an object or service has any meaning; *value* is a mutual subject of transacting participants. The free rational participants will decide on the worth matter of anything according to their own circumstances, also the rationality of their judgments is based on their private circumstances, in most of the cases the circumstances of the transacting participants may not be identical thus value judgments might vary. Though their value judgments may or may not be the same but exchange will happen only because of their circumstances. The agreement to exchange will set an exchange-value of the produce for that instance.

In brief, ETC places focus on the *exchange-value*, set for the object or service at the particular moment of the event of exchange; the *exchange-value* has a limited life that may vary after the event as everything is changing around including the circumstances of the participants. By the way, the *exchange-value* has nothing to do with the *exchange theory of value* and shall not be confused in any way. Principally, *value* and *exchange-value* are two unlike concepts, *individualistic* and *mutualistic*, in that order. All existing *theories on value* are partially true to a degree but not helpful in bringing a consensus on the matter of *value* but *exchange-value is a fact not a theory* and therefore the most relevant truth of economics.

An absolute truth is not a property of any particular doctrine, the *exchange-value* is an absolute fact or truth as evident by its occurrence and no theoretical doubts can be created on this materialized and witnessed fact. But this can't be assured for a theory. For instance, *the cost-of-production theory of value* may be related in one system of accounting like in capitalism, but the theory is irrelevant in Chinese model of costing used by a large segment of production under government enterprises. The point here is that the philosophical base of an idea must be universal otherwise its science is not perfect. If we label economics as a subject of social science then it shall have universal philosophical base and not biased to some doctrine like capitalism or else. The economic theory of circumstances (ETC) fulfills this prerequisite.

A theoretical premise based on some verifiable facts is more convincing than a theoretical premise based on abstract ideas. The *value* in existing economic theories of value is an abstract idea creating a double jeopardy in the understanding of subjects related to value since both, the theory and the focal substance of theory, are conjectural. In the case of ETC, the *exchange-event* and the *exchange-value* are verifiable facts and the premise of theory is based on circumstances of the participants, thus there is enough real substance for the science of economics to study economic equilibrium and justice to transacting participants. The economic equilibrium and the economic justice are seen only in the context of the circumstances of participants therefore one cannot subtract economic agents from the sphere of any study, making economics a perfect social science discipline.

The basic hydrogen-oxygen structure of water does not change wherever you go from country to country on this planet irrespective of any political system that is in place there. The scientists working on the subject of water across the world understand water alike and take benefit from each others' efforts and research on the matter of water. This universality in material sciences produces universal benefits for the inhabitants of the planet. However, when it comes to the social sciences like economics, unfortunately there are no common structures or grounds for social scientists and theorists to understand social subjects in that way of universal acceptance. The concepts of justice whether it be social or economic justice is therefore limited to a particular way of thinking e.g., socialistic and capitalistic or else, it also implies that the meaning of justice are different in different belief systems. Indeed, it is not only the concept of justice but social and moral standards might vary by a significant degree in different doctrines.

Like the molecular structure of water, circumstances of an economic entity are the microscopic structure of the body but having too many atomic elements unlike just two in water. We can draw another parallel here, the molecular structure of water reacts to molecular structures of other materials in some given conditions, similarly the circumstances of an economic entity may interacts with the circumstances of another entity in a given situation resulting in an exchange-event.

Revisiting Economic Justice

In modern law and economics, the justice is a vague concept; more focus is given on economic analysis and economic efficiency in a contractual event of exchange for any basis sought in making a judicial, analytical or technical decision. Although this derivative justice is not much convincing to a large segment of its critics for other reasons they have, but in my view, the vagueness of justice has its basic reason in the vague definition of economic activity itself that confines modern economic thinking to production, distribution and consumption activities. These are secondary level subjects by nature as recognized in our sense of economic studies while justice is a primary level issue that may not be defined at any lesser levels. Another reason for vague concept of justice in modern economic discipline is - economic analysis or economic efficiency estimations are reliant upon *assumptions* and *predefined rationality* expected from economic agents, where both considerations are inconclusive therefore when source is unreliable than any derivative justice may not be convincing as well.

For instance, the decision-making attitude from any economic agent is believed to benefit optimally from an economic interaction regardless of any other logic that he may possess in his very own circumstances to act differently. This universalizing of behavior about human beings as being the rational maximizers and act always for their individual and maximum satisfaction, is not a universal truth in any way. These partial truths of imperfect assumptions are unhelpful for the science of economics. Mostly assumptive economic theories, in point of fact, are not helping the science of economics just because of lacking universal truth in focal subject, and examples of very popular economic theories utilize assumptive data and variables to prove respective idea.

The dilemma with modern economic thinking is that it's caged in production, distribution and consumption activities only and making economic justice a second tier subject. Justice is to whom? Obviously, there can't be a second thought but to economic entities (person or business) and the society. Then, justice is to come from where? Logically, it is irrefutable that the justice has to come only from the economic interaction among the entities. If justice is meant for economic entities when they interact then the most important thing to consider is the satisfaction and contentment of those interacting economic entities. It is only justice in any affair that can satisfy the participants, while secondary subjects like economic efficiency, welfare, cost benefits, distributive allocation of resources etc. etc. are actually managerial subjects. Justice is a primary theme of ETC as it thinks about the circumstances of the participants, insisting to treat them for their satisfaction. Since each participant having exclusive circumstances therefore, economic justice may have different meanings for each of them.

Rethinking Economic Equilibrium

The condition of economic equilibrium is defined as the balance of economic forces in present mainstream economics; we know this stance on the subject as the dominant statement however the definition is facing significant criticism but no alternative description. The economic thinking presented in this script is distinct at the root and where since the prime subject of study and analysis for any such matter is the exchange event, thus conditions of economic equilibrium are distinctive too.

In view of the essential premise of 'economic theory of circumstances', the condition of equilibrium has its basis in the objective close of exchange-event i.e., when the purposes of the participants, as expected by them, are realized effectively to their satisfaction, and for that reason the prerequisites of an objective close are set in the following rules:

1) All exchange-values to be transferred, from one to the other participant(s) in an exchange-event, must either be come-at-able (existing, to hand, accessible, attainable) from within the event or to be generated by the event *ipso facto*.

2) If exchange-values are come-at-able from within the event then the transfers of exchange-values must be equal. The first preferential equivalence method is by social standards if applicable and then by mutual negotiation.

3) However, if one or more exchange-values are to be generated by the event then the equivalence of exchange-values at the time of transfer is not a condition, however it is must to agree on some determination of exchange-values whatsoever.

The rules are apparently simple yet cover the whole economic sphere of exchange-events. The philosophy behind is very simple too i.e., all exchange-values shall either exist at the time of the exchange or generated by the event to settle down the promises of delivery with certainty. It further implies that no uncertain objective is contextualized and no objective is made external to the exchange-event.

The equivalence of existential exchange-values is a natural demand since no one would like to exchange unequal exchange-values in a normal state of mind and the equivalence will definitely ensure the satisfaction of the participants; however the condition of equivalence does not apply if any participant is in volunteering or altruistic state of mind.

The equivalence may not be a condition when one or more exchange-values are to be generated by the event; firstly, since the exchange-value is not yet in existence and secondly, since the contribution of participants in generating the exchange-value(s) may be unequal and thus the equivalence is not a demand of participants as well. In such a case, naturally the participants will be satisfied on the agreement of exchange-values as per their respective contribution in generating the same.

So, unlike the balancing of vague economic forces of demand and supply, satisfying the circumstances of the participants for their hopes from the exchange-event is not a vague or indefinable thing. Still, the philosophical impasse of 'invisible hands' is not worked out which I guess was a cover up of eighteenth century economist, Adam Smith, for some missing dot in his thoughts on demand and supply for its balancing by some unknown self-regulating phenomenon. The balancing of vague economic forces is in the air while satisfying economic agents for their circumstances is on ground. All factors i.e., circumstances of the participants, exchange-event, real exchange-values, inputs from economic agents, the applicable social standards if any, mutual negotiations or else matters of exchange are all existent here within the event; a right course of action between these factors to result in the satisfaction of the participants is thus conceived as economic equilibrium. Not the balancing of economic forces but satisfaction of economic agents is the condition of economic equilibrium in ETC.

Anomaly in exchange-event

Generally, the majority of people are reasonable and decent enough to deal honestly, they respect standard practices and norms of society; by and large people are not bad but their circumstances can be. When people perform justly and fulfill their commitments timely as expected from them then everyone is satisfied with the results of economic interaction. This is a normal state of affairs, sought too in creating a happy and contented people society – the prime objective of all economies.

The participants indeed have few expectations from the exchange-events they are taking part in; such as the creditor would be hoping some profit from a 'for profit' type of exchange-event; the debtor may or may not be looking for a profit but would have other expectations. The expectations are precisely the evidence of current state of circumstances and the modes of actions of the participants. A condition of anomaly will develop in the event of exchange when expectations of one or more participants are not met as were desired or expected or as one could satisfy with. The anomaly will always have some reason, internal or external in origin. Internally, when some unjust is done by any or all participant(s) to others in the activity, or some mishap occurs to the activity itself. Externally, since we live in a constantly changing world thus probabilities of change in exterior circumstances do exists that may affect the participants or economic process with unexpected results.

Normally, anomalies in exchange-events are not by design but uncalled-for irregularities having any reason from inside or outside of the event. That said, in case of a compromised situation though, an anomaly may be introduced by agreement or by design. On the time line of economic interaction, the anomaly can occur at the start of exchange-event (e.g., for a reason of neglect or concealment of private information by participants, or if a force or influence is used, directly or indirectly, to achieve an intended purpose or to exploit counterparts vulnerability, or the absence of an adequate option may force to compromise etc. etc.); also when the exchange-event prolongs over a period of time, a later on change occurs in the initial circumstances of economic agents, or there goes something wrong with the process or with externally connected circumstances - making anomaly condition to the event, the anomaly reasons likely are:

1. Misleading or concealing the facts

2. Using direct or indirect forceful leverage

3. Exploiting anyone's vulnerabilities

4. Demanding or agreeing to deliver anything that is external to the exchange-event.

5. Change in circumstances as stated above.

The anomaly is by information, influence, ingenuity, irrationality or impromptu, if we label above reasons. The first three reasons are hidden; last one is a matter of destiny; anomaly by irrationality is the reason which is possible out of contractual terms like in lending and sale contracts, our subject query, let's look in to it.

The rationality or the rational behavior of economic agents has no universal monotony for the reason that the rationality comes from beliefs of economic agents having some reasons of beliefs in their religion, routine practices in society or else living values; these domains are so diverse across the regions that all rational actors may not make same decision in exactly the same given set of economic conditions. We shall not challenge the religious beliefs of any economic entity however it will not be amiss to study beliefs on 'routine practices' or other living values that do not relate to religion.

In above view, there are two probabilities for having an irrational behavior by an economic agent i.e., while acting against the known reason of belief in religion, or when involved in a 'routine practice' that itself has no valid reason.

The second one is quite interesting since supposedly the rational behavior of economic agent is grown up in his belief on 'routine practice' as everyone is doing that. However, if there is no valid reason of the practice then effectively his 'rational behavior' may be 'irrational'.

In perspective of subject query, we have exactly this situation as 'lending on interest' is a 'routine practice' but there is no convincing reason for the validity of the practice except for few skewed theories. The query says what is irrational in this practice that is different from the practice of Murabaha financing? Though a number of dissimilarities have been shown earlier in the script, yet in this last leg of presentation, we may reaffirm the differences from economics only. Even though, ETC thinking is fundamentally different from conventional beliefs, however we will find irrationality using realistic social and economic arguments acceptable to any way of thinking. Primarily, the search of cause will focus the circumstances of the participants. A relevant matter to identify the modes (PWO, BBO) of economic entities in an exchange-event may first be discussed before that.

Identifying the mode of action

Why is it necessary to identify the mode of action of every participant? The common good of society is the answer in short; one possible source of the common good is economic interactions. Since everyone would like to be treated justly as per his own circumstances therefore he must treat his counterparts according to his circumstances. The circumstances of an economic entity are characterized by his mode of action therefore it is required to identify the mode of counterpart to deal with him in a socially correct way. This may sound very simple by current economics but the matter of fact is that this basic procedure will improve the economic efficiency of transactions in an unprecedented way for reasons we can advocate. It is obvious, there are just two modes of actions in ETC and every economic agent would naturally be in one of the two. However, despite this simple binary probability, it is necessary to identify the true mode of action so that the one must know the other to deal with him suitably. In social relationship, responding to the counterpart in a way respecting and accepting his state of affairs will foster contentment and satisfaction, thus will result in the common good to the society. Additionally, this is actually much required conduct too from the participant to avoid or reduce the chances of anomaly at the start of the exchange-event.

The question may arise, how to identify the modes? There may be several methods for the social inquiry to identify the mode of action like by any acceptable way of exchanging information, by knowing the personal or business history and current standing worth or else. It may even be made mandatory by law to unveil this fact, adequate disclosure values can be set up by economic authorities for the purpose. The purpose to emphasize on this requisite is to remove the uncertainty at start of the exchange-event since otherwise economic justice or equilibrium may be compromised at the very first step. That said, on the other hand, there are few indicators that may self-identify the mode of action without any efforts or rules. For instance, if an economic body is willing to purchase anything of general well-off quality (e.g., a car, house etc.), this will make obvious his mode of action as BBO; likewise, when a debtor engages in an augmentation or creation type of economic activity will imply that the body is in BBO mode, most probably.

If no self-identifying means or signal is available like when the debtor demands the objects of consumption or the money where it is not possible for the creditor to decipher the mode of action of the debtor then some method will be required to verify this prerequisite fact. The professional people can find several possible ways to investigate the fact using many techniques. A basic or broader segregation is though easier as there are few basic correlations of modes, as below:

Table 11 : Few correlations of PWO & BBO

Indicators for the	Indications (if)	Modes
Nature of Object	Non-Negotiable like Money Negotiable like Commodities Having well-off/prosperous quality	PWO, BBO PWO, BBO BBO
Number of Object(s) in exchange-event	One Two or More (if being traded)	PWO, BBO BBO
Type of Activity	Creation Augmentation Transference Diminution	BBO BBO PWO, BBO PWO, BBO

By not identifying the modes of actions, the event of exchange may not break off but the expectations and satisfaction of participants from exchange-event may be compromised and chances of unwarranted anomaly might increase.

Relevance of ETC in Debt case

There is an utterly well conceived and coherent kind of economic thinking behind the formation of ETC; the central idea was to develop a simple and philosophical premise for every principle or statement with a concept of totality, means once a statement is orchestrated then nothing of that subject shall be left out. This approach is vital to see economics as science of universal reasons within social spectrum. For instance the presentation of the 'natural law of profit' is very simple but no one can refute its basic premise confirming its universality. Then, realizing the inadequate definition of economic activity in today's economic thinking, a novel definition of 'economic activity' is given, again having convincing universality for the underlying reasons. The incoherent current categories of economic activities are suggested to be replaced with perfectly relevant new classification scheme. There are more conceptual statements that one may find in this script. Briefly, it was intended to uphold the universality of reasons to demonstrate the discipline of economics as a science rather than just a hypothetical or conjectural thinking as employed in most economic theories.

The only demerit of this approach is - it is so simple that it has more chances to be neglected for the reasons of its simplicity than professional class of theories. The ETC is applicable to all economic entities in real terms without any assumptions, where benefit or gain is not seen in isolation by selfish individualistic angles but in mutual or communal perspective. This is because, gain or profit for one has to come from other entity in the event of exchange therefore gain cannot be an exclusive or private matter in social relationships thus it is not sensible to ignore the circumstances of the source from where profit or gain has to come. This simple approach also implies that all economic entities in an exchange-event are relevant economically for any sort of study such as economic justice or economic equilibrium.

Let's apply the concepts offered hitherto including 'economic theory of circumstances (ETC)' to the credit transactions in question. There we have the creditor and the debtor; their modes of actions; the exchange-values and number of objects in transactions; the type of economic activities or the one undertaken with the credit; in view of their relations and selection of these variables; to determine economic distinctive traits.

The creditor (for his ability to extend credit and his intent of profit) shall always be operating in BBO mode therefore we only need to identify the mode of debtor in order to find the exact pair of modes. Even though, any of the two situations i.e., PWO-BBO or BBO-BBO is possible when they meet up; the motive of creditor will be satisfied when he meets up with an economic entity having the same BBO mode because debtor with this mode will only have the ability to offer profit to the creditor. Hence, for the profit motive of the debtor, a BBO-BBO match will be hitch-free and there will be no anomaly initially.

On the other hand, when a potential debtor gets in touch with the creditor, the debtor may either disclose its intent and circumstances with him like what use or activity is intended with the credit obtained, or can just show off his mode in any way. An offer to buy a well-off kind of thing like house or a car, or a thing to resell will show off his mode as BBO. When it is established that the debtors' mode of action is also BBO, then both will only need to decide on terms for exchanging the objects and will secure their respective gain or expectations in the objects they will receive. Apparently and positively, there is no 'anomaly' in notice at the beginning of such exchange-event as both carry BBO mode and there are minimum of two objects involved. The only possibility of 'anomaly' may either be hidden initially or thereafter a subsequent change of circumstances of participants, economic process or the connected settings. In initial phase of the exchange-event, the economic equilibrium exists and no anomaly found; later abnormality cannot be ruled out in this time bound event, if such anomaly occurs subsequently, some re-thinking to the economic interaction will be necessary to reestablish the missing economic balance or equilibrium (in original Islamic injunctions, this re-thinking is actually demanded, by re-negotiating the terms to adjust accordingly).

When both (creditor and debtor) are in BBO mode and the numbers of objects involved in exchange-event are two or more then we do not expect any anomaly at the start of the event. They will ensure their respective gains in respective objects of exchange to them as they mutually agreed to transfer. It may be remembered as a universal principle that a gain, benefit or advantage is built and transferred through the object(s) present in the event of exchange, money or else. The objects of exchange serve as carrier of gain, benefit or advantage.

If credit is made out of money and the same has to be returned to the creditor (i.e., there is only one object in exchange-event); this is really interesting situation since there can only be one gain if there is any (because there is only one object of exchange involved). If both are in BBO mode, will imply that both will be looking for some profit from their mutual interaction, in this case it's essential that an economic activity of creation or augmentation class is undertaken with the credit to satisfy the profit expectations of two economic entities. On the contrary, if no gainful activity is assumed with the credit, will imply that the debtor's mode of action is PWO, it will further signify that there is no profit on offer from the debtor to the creditor in this BBO-PWO setting. An anomaly will be introduced in such event of exchange if profit for the creditor is secured or inflicted by any means or in any way. It is inevitable to identify the mode of the debtor to study economic factors.

In ETC, the possibility of subsequent changes in the circumstances of the participants is taken seriously if the exchange-event is lasting over a period of time like in loan or credit deals. There is a possibility of change in initial circumstances of one or both entities (creditor and debtor). That is – an initial BBO-BBO interaction may convert to a PWO-BBO or PWO-PWO relation or an initial BBO-PWO interaction may be converted to a BBO-BBO or PWO-PWO relation by such happenings.

If the creditors' exclusive purpose of extending the credit is to get some profit from the transaction then in order to breed the condition of economic equilibrium, it is must for him to ensure that the credit is used in a gainful economic activity or in other word the debtor is also carrying BBO mode; if such assurance is not made or knowing that the economic activity does not fall in gainful category then the disturbing anomaly is surely stipulated at the inception of the transaction because there is no source of profit exist.

As said earlier, the query is for technical comparison of two types of transactions where interest is manifest as a gain in transaction involving money only while the profit is manifest also as a gain in the other transaction involving money and some other object. In Islamic way of thinking profit is legitimate but interest is not, thus what the difference in two gains is, such query is placed by conventional thinking who consider interest as legal gain. There are many theories in western world trying to explore the justification for interest e.g., productivity associated with capital; reason of abstinence in saving capital for lending; the time-preference reward since a man prefers present consumption as compared to the future one or the preference of having a sum of money now than to have some in future; interest as reward for the productive use of the capital equal to the marginal productivity; interest as the reward of not hoarding or consuming the capital but investing. All these theories on interest are criticized in the western world with very valid objections, though the critics have valid criticism but even they accept the system of interest despite their dissatisfaction with given justifications. In the presence of such exposing criticism, it is rather better to leave these "sorry-theories" on interest without any further possible dissection. We have already built a case to see the thin line of segregation between two transactions in socio-economic context and will answer the query and the earlier withheld explanations.

The Pre-Answering Stuff

Extra Liability

In the table of two debts portrayal example, we had a column of 'extra liability'; it was not explained earlier but here only. The economy, irrespective of any system of belief, is built as a matter of fact, exclusively by the incidents of exchange-events; the causes of event are in the circumstances of the participants and an accurate handling of these circumstances is required. The seed of justice or injustice, regardless of the intentions of the participants, is implanted then and there, concurrently with the event of exchange. The socio-economic justice comes by the equilibrium state of exchange-event and injustice by the disequilibrium state.

In our economic thinking, the equilibrium condition is when the purposes of the participants are satisfied as expected by them; few rules were also defined for the condition of equilibrium. In the case of 'sale of a thing', no matter whether it is on spot or by credit, no matter whether the money or the negotiable article of trade is credited in the credit sale; since there is one negotiable article of trade, at least, thus equivalence of negotiated exchange-values is verified by the two-sided offer and acceptance procedure. This is very common sense of a thing - all exchangeable goods must be assessed equal for a valid exchange; why two shall exchange unequal exchange-values with free will in a sale. When they can settle the price (exchange-value) of negotiable thing to define equivalence legally and are free to set the terms including any time period for the delivery of respective exchange-values then these firm exchange-values will be come-at-able in the course of the event. Hence, the rule one and two of equilibrium conditions are satisfied in the 'sale of a thing' and thus economic equilibrium is established. Both participants will have their objectives achieved at the close of the event ensuring justice from the event as well.

On the other hand for the second transaction case of 'lending on interest' event; let us see this in view of the conditions of economic equilibrium. The first rule says that the exchange-values shall be come-at-able or to be generated in the course of event. Here, the first rule is partial true i.e., one exchange-value (principal amount) is available in the event that can be transferred to the borrower or even back to the creditor in few situations. The come-at-able condition may even be true, in full, if the debtor is in a position to return the principal with Interest i.e., the first rule is positive. However in that case the subsequent condition is applicable demanding the exchange-values to be transferred must be equal. It is certainly not happening therefore the condition of economic equilibrium is not conformed. Secondly, as this is simple lending contract, not associated with any gainful economic activity, implies that Interest will not be generated by the event as well therefore the non-equivalence may not be justified as stated in third rule stipulated for the equilibrium conditions.

Practically, interest is made external to the lending event i.e., a part of the exchange-value is not come-at-able in the course of the event; interest is making two exchange-values unequal as well; interest is creating an 'extra liability' on the borrower who after discharging the 'extra liability' will go permanently deficient by that much of private worth since he had received nothing in return of it (i.e., equal to interest). If we remember the earlier example of two debts portrayal (Table 10), all deficiencies of successive borrowers when added will create an implicit debt liability to the shared economy, of a size which is more than the principal amount that was lent initially. The shared economy (anthology of individual economies of borrowers in example) will go in a net deficiency equal to the Interest sum of all the borrowers there, the balance of the shared economy is disturbed. The first disequilibrium in *lending on interest* exchange-event has created subsequent disequilibrium in the societal economy. When two exchange-values are not equal in any transaction whatsoever then it is obvious that an extra transfer of wealth has happened in favour of the one who gets extra - lender in this case. The "sorry theories" are one-sided considering extra as utter right of capital and do not consider its impact on the individual or societal economy or the social aspects. The 'extra liability' creates economic disequilibrium in individual and societal economies. Therefore, despite having identical figures in table - two gains and debts are not equal in economic thinking.

The Argument of Natural Selection

Access to money is the right of people when they have the need for any purpose even to survive or intend to do some economic activity etc.; loan is one form that

188

can honour this right of access to money. On the other hand, it is undeniable right of the lender to have his money back as agreed. Is the interest also a right of the lender and people accepting it without annoyance? Let us do a litmus test for this question; say if two options are available to the borrower i.e., to get the money that he wants - with or without Interest, with or without any 'extra liability' – every borrower will rationally pick the option of 'without Interest or without extra liability'. Even if the same lender, asking for Interest on money, himself needs money to borrow and is offered with the same choices, definitely his selection will be the same. There is no reason why a borrower in his vigilant state of mind and in the presence of an option to have the same money without interest, will select the other. Logically, no one would like to apportion very minimal of his exchange-value just for nothing, this is just too natural to be refuted. There is no logic or assertion in my notice from conventional advocates that can favour the case of lending on interest with natural arguments and reasoning. It is actually the system of money that is designed purposely, eliminating the choice of having money without interest; the nature is suppressed by the removal of first option and people are in fact forced to use the only option around.

Money if invested and generates more money than it can be shared by the partakers and people agree to this sharing logically; but when money is lent only and is not put to generate more money than people by nature do not want to pay more than what they had borrowed; is it not true and verifies this stance that when it comes to you, you also prefer what others choose, then why we cannot make it a principle for all – money shall not demand interest by lending? This is the nature (*fitrah*) of human beings. Obviously, no one can deny the right of claiming the principal but at the same time no one actually wants to accept the demand of interest at free will of choice. This human nature is applauded in the Holy Quran with a force of law i.e., you can just have your principal sums only[11]; the rest is illegal in Islam. The supporters of *interest* ask - why someone would lend his money without having any benefit from it and consequently the borrower who needs money will face the hard time without having it. The reason is not true, because the need only needs money and if the option without interest is available to the needy, obviously he will go for that. In fact, the conventional argument is not sympathizing with the borrower but with interest based system of money which cannot survive without its forced implementation. The return on money is just rational but only from gainful activity, this is possible from an alternate system by a blend of gainful and no gain economic activities arranged in some fashion, but such financial institution are possible if and only if, the facts of economics will define the financing logic and not the finance defining the economics.

---

[11] *Quran 2:279*

Economic Distinction

In mainstream and heretical economic theories, the allocation of resources to the people in a society or to various uses is a frequently referred subject. Though, such theories, particularly in mainstream economics, are based on perfect information scenarios and stretch arguments to the extremes within the spectrum of an assumed situation, however the projection of thoughts is mostly restricted in one way or the other. Such as the famous Pareto efficiency or Pareto optimality theory argues that the resource allocation is adequate, as long as, if one entity gets better-off without making any other entity worse-off and the perfect efficiency reaches at point where further reallocation of resource to make an entity better-off, will be at the expense of another turning worse-off. The concept seems artistic but vague and may not cover the entire system of any economy.

Having said that and surely the Pareto theorems are quite challengeable in view of our economic thinking, still for its limited relevance to the context of query, we may explore our cases for Pareto efficiencies. We have two Pareto scenarios; a 'lending on interest' case where we have two agents and one good; then in 'Murabaha financing' case, we have two agents and two goods, and both are individual exchanges. The numbers will differ if we apply Pareto theory on earlier two debts portrayal of twenty transactions. We may see Pareto efficiencies in individual lending and trade contracts.

Pareto Efficiency, ETC and Lending on Interest

Let us consider an economy of two persons and one resource i.e., a lender, a borrower and the money. In its existing state of single resource economy (no choice or preference), any allocation of resource is efficient only if no reallocation of resource occurs in single resource economy as conceded by the Pareto efficiency concept. Simultaneously, when the 'lending on interest' event is started, reallocation of resource occurs in the economy. The Pareto theorem only talks about the allocation of resources therefore by that approach the lender is now worse-off as compared to its previous allocative status while the borrower becomes better-off instantly. Since one entity has become worse-off, thus as said by Pareto theorem, the contract of lending in its initial outlook, is not Pareto efficient.

In economic thinking of ETC, the lender does not go to a worse-off state just by lending but only by meeting losses or when his store depletes below current level of consumption. If he faces such situations then he will not like to lend money rationally. Therefore, according to ETC, the lender has not gone worse-off initially and the lending is adequate in its initial outlook if we apply Pareto theorem using ETC definition of worse-off.

Let's skip the lending period of contract since Pareto rules are relevant only when some change in resource allocation occurs; whereas the period is not ignorable in ETC owing to the difference of basic economic ideas between the two economic thinking i.e., conventional pitch is materialistic whereas ETC is humanistic.

At the time when the 'lending on interest' event is concluded, again reallocation of resource has occurred in the economy. Now the lender has become better-off and the borrower worse-off because of transferring the money with interest to the lender. Since the borrower has become worse-off, thus as said by Pareto theorem, the contract of lending in its final outlook, is also not Pareto efficient.

If we evaluate the close of event by ETC thinking i.e., when the borrower returns money along with interest, he goes in a permanent deficiency state as he loses his private worth equal to interest because he did not get anything in return of that. Therefore the borrower is in a declining or worse-off state now after the settlement of loan plus interest, in view of ETC thinking.

The 'lending on interest' transaction is not Pareto efficient, in its initial occurrence when the time bound event is started and also at the close of the event, as per the Pareto Efficiency theorems. Moreover, even when we apply ETC definitions of economic status to Pareto Efficiency, the 'lending on interest' is adequate initially but is not Pareto efficient at the close of event. In brief, the said transaction is not Pareto Efficient.

Pareto Efficiency, ETC and Murabaha Financing

Let us consider an economy of two persons and two goods i.e., a seller, a buyer, an article and the money. The buyer wants the article and the seller is looking for money. In its existing state of economy, the allocation of resources is not efficient as the two persons do not own what they want, a relocation of resources if occurs such that buyer gets the article and seller gets money, only then the situation will revert to Pareto efficient. When 'Murabaha Financing' event is started, the article is reallocated to the buyer who becomes better-off; but the seller does not become worse-off since he did not want the article. The situation is adequate as per Pareto theorem since no one gets worse-off initially.

In economic thinking of ETC as well, the seller does not go to a worse-off state since he has the capacity to extend the credit and exhibiting BBO mode. Therefore, even ETC thinking and definitions are applied to initial status of the transaction; the situation is adequate as per Pareto theorem. I am using the word 'adequate' to refer to a situation which is basically moving towards a Pareto efficient condition or sensing/exhibiting Pareto improvement.

A reallocation of resource occurs when the buyer has settled its dues against Murabaha Financing; now the seller becomes better-off without turning the buyer to a worse-off state simply because buyer had no want of money but the article which he already had, or the buyer had preference for the article over the money. Thus the two, buyer and seller, have become better-off by respective reallocation of resources happened by the event of Murabaha Financing that is ended with Pareto efficient allocation of resources in the economy.

Therefore, the first economic distinction is evident if we see the query from mainstream economics of today i.e., when we apply Pareto Efficiency theorems to cases in hand; the lending on interest is not Pareto Efficient while Murabaha Financing is.

Exclusivity of ETC

Though, we just observed that lending on interest is not an efficient transaction whereas the credit in trade is efficient in view of mainstream economics, however the query is far more serious than an efficiency issue. It is a matter of legitimacy – why the lending on interest is an illegal act in Islamic belief but credit in trade with integral profit is not? The answer must be distinctive to the satisfaction of economic intellect. It is imperative to briefly go over the leading economic thinking that have been influencing the societies in the recent past to this age just to re-emphasize the exclusivity of ETC which is though already demonstrated throughout this script as well. Let's limit this review only to original economic ideas that turned into economic systems of capitalism (free market economy) and communism.

The 'subprime mortgage crisis of 2008' is a typical instance of failure of mainstream economics doctrine. The asset bubble created in housing market was burst exposing the weak point of capitalism i.e., the artificial profit. Since the happening of the financial crisis, there are several myths and guess works to find what actually caused the crisis, so many theories have been floating around the world to find the reasons as the crisis had a global impact; however in our economic thinking, the one and only underlying reason is the 'artificial profit' making modus operandi. The 'invisible hand' did not turn up to self-regulate the housing market which was being built on inflated demand and supply of single asset based multiple artificial securities.

When a house is financed, naturally the profit of the financier is built in the receivables from the borrower i.e., the profit and the source of profit are determined. Principally, the financier is free to share his profit with anyone he likes. He can assign the sales proceeds or the debt paper by discounting the same or else method of selling at less than its face value – that's the only way of sharing the profit. However, any extra or premium on top of the receivables or debt does not exist at the time of reselling contract since the price of the house is not re-negotiated thus it's an artificial or speculative profit. It's not something very difficult to understand that all artificial profits in each derivative selling will add up as an extra liability or deficit to the societal economy.

The societal economy was gone in a sheer deficit by the sum of all artificial profits built in every reselling of the debts on premium. In order to offset this deficit, an equal had to come from somewhere to restore balance and to save the economy from a total collapse. The Fed and US government managed bailout packages and few regulations to settle the dust of deficit. Though, despite going through this traumatic crisis, the proponents of mainstream economics have not considered the factor of artificial profit as cause of the event, perhaps for the reasons if they do - the whole system of interest would be distrusted. There is a natural segregation of real and artificial profit no matter if they accept it or not. In real natural economic thinking, a profit is legal if and only if it conforms to the natural law of profit i.e., *the profit is a construct of time and economic activity*. The selling of house is an economic activity where a change of value occurs, with thanks to the negotiable object, the house, but the selling of debt is not an economic activity since no change of value can occur in effect as debt papers or receivables have fixed exchange-values. The selling of debt is not an economic activity even in mainstream economics by its own definition of economic activity. The artificial profit making modes operandi is the weak point of capitalism, evidently proved in this crisis. The phenomenal feature of artificial profit may prove fatal to any capitalist economy; acts as a catalyst of wealth concentration and the capitalization of resources in few hands; that is what the capitalism is all about.

Any profit that does not conform to the natural law of profit is illegal; the premium on debt instruments or the interest in lending contracts are the artificial profit since no economic activity happens in these exchanges. If profit does not exist technically and naturally, then it may only be imposed by force or using some deception. Though, using force or deception may not be approved in any social code but the divine codes are explicit in its prohibition as in Islam, Christianity, and Judaism or in other religions. The interest is though prohibited in all divine religions however in Islam it is more explicit and better defined.

On the other hand, communism in my view is the extreme form of capitalism if we see it for its ability to capitalize the resources; a communist government will take control of all the resources in the economy but the ownership remains hypothetical, that's the difference in capitalism and communism – capitalism exercises the control in distributed fashion and allows ownership of resources. The extreme nature of communism along with hypothetical ownership of resources in the hands of few government functionaries is the weak spot of the system and was the reason of the short life it had, in my view. Then in communist economic thinking, profit is a taboo thing that is tantamount to suppressing the very nature of the human beings. The current state of once communist countries is enough to understand that the economic thinking of communism was not convincing.

The exclusivity of ETC is that it considers real profit at its logical place, defines it by a universal natural law; whereas in capitalism, there is no distinction between a real and artificial profit, as a matter of fact rather, most of the financial operations in capitalist system employ artificial profit; lastly in communism, they are against the profit, real or artificial. But how the 'artificial profit' erodes the legitimacy of transaction? Simply because it does not exist therefore including this in any contract invalidates the contract. Its non-existence has been demonstrated all through the script.

Ethical Judgment

Increasing or decreasing the price of any negotiable article of trade, is an undeniable right of the seller and his offer is only subject to the counterparts' acceptance to buy, the profit he makes or the loss he bears in doing so, is his personal judgment and intentional act having his own economic reasons as per his circumstances and subjective acumen. Since there is no breach of societal norm in doing so, therefore his act of setting the price is justified legally and ethically.

On the contrary, increasing or decreasing the price of a non-negotiable item like money is not the right of the lending creditor; it violates the societal norms thus unjustified legally and ethically.

Answers to the query

In previous chapter of 'what exactly is the query', we outlined four variants of the query; the first two queries are from conventional minds while the next two are by Islamic misunderstanding on the subject of Riba. The answer to each variant of the query is given separately.

In Sales Context

The first argument was based on the fact that barren money does not produce any gain or profit rather it has to be employed to earn profit; everyone irrespective of his belief system, conventional, Islamic or else, accepts this intrinsic feature of money. However logically there must be some philosophy of generating profit where money can be engaged. In coherence with few facts, an undeniable natural law of profit was introduced, saying that "*Profit is a function (construct) of time and economic activity*". This is universal law applicable to money too. Pursuant to this law, an *economic activity* is essential to generate some profit. Then owing to our dissatisfaction with the conventional definition of economic activity as it was lacking a conceptual statement and not coherent even with given classes therefore we also defined what an economic activity is in our economic perspective.

The conventionalists call interest to be the profit; if we analyze the contract of 'lending on interest' in view of the natural law of profit, we see that either it is mere a simple act of exchange without an economic activity or even if it is linked to an activity, its contractual role is limited to the input stage of the activity and has no further contractual involvement. If lending the money is not further associated to the economic process where the change of value (real or perceptive) actually occurs or where profit is actually built, if built, then fixing the profit when it does not exists is insane and irrational act. The profit is forced to exist where it does not and cannot exist, therefore illegal.

The act of 'lending on interest' does not comply with the natural law of profit therefore any gain constructed in this course of act or exchange cannot be regarded as real profit that nature demands. The gain in 'lending on interest' is an artificial profit, ethically and legally not approved but only by the force of law or deception.

Whereas '*Murabaha* Financing', is always attached to some economic activity where profit is constructed and is available for sharing or distribution; it complies and coheres with the natural law of profit, thus the implicit gain is real profit by the very reason of law. The interest (*added to the loan or principal*) **is not a valid profit** while the gain (*added to the cost*) **is a valid profit**. This position is very simple and clear, if someone does not accept the reason of law or the law of profit then one must present some other law of profit to refute it, only an argument of this strength can challenge this reasoning or the law.

In Debt's Perspective

The other underlined criticism within queries relates to the concept of 'time value of money' where tweaking of thoughts on both sides, conventional and Islamic, is required in our economic thinking. In our view, *there is a time value of every value that has an exchange-value*; this is because every exchange-value has a life implying that some change of value is occurring inside the value itself or outside the value in relation to other values. In this context of exchange-value-life which is dependent on time, there is a time value of every value, for reasons of changing the value inside the value itself, let's call it an *endogenous time value* of value or a relative change of value to call it an *exogenous time value* of value.

The change of value may be either way, up or down, slow of fast – may be so slow as in decades and so fast in few seconds; changes are reflected in exchange-value of the value. The perishable values have endogenous time value however money does not fall in this class. Since the negotiable values have their price set in terms of money therefore money cannot have exogenous time value relative to any negotiable value. However, money of one genre may have a relative exchange-value with another genre of money therefore money may have an exogenous time value in relation to other money.

The query (in debt's perspective) insists that 'time value of money' is a definite reason of similarity in the gain and profit constructed in two credits extended by loan and trade transactions respectively.

The concept of 'time value of money' in conventional money system is somewhat like the 'chicken or the egg' dilemma. The time value of money is set by interest on money and then interest is justified by saying 'money has a time value'. The proof is, if you make Interest rate zero in conventional formulas that are used to calculate present and future values of money, then the present value (PV) and the future value (FV)[12] of money will be the same, no difference in money values over time is noticed, thus no 'time value of money'. When Interest on money is not justified by the natural law of profit then *it makes no sense to justify the 'time value of money' which is defined by interest.*

In reality thus, the argument of '*time value of money defined by interest*' to claim the similarity in two debts is not a valid argument because there is no endogenous or exogenous time value in same genre of money. This does not mean that time has no value, but in fact *time is value* rather the most invaluable thing in our belief. On the other hand, if money was employed in an economic activity, it will take some time to produce an output. If a profit is generated from the activity then any part of the profit may be allocated to money input as share i.e., the investor gets more money than what he had put in,

---

[12] $FV = PV \times (1+i)^n$

implying that money gets more money by the amount of his share in profit. We can attribute this increase of money towards time i.e., profit over a definite period of time thus there may be a '*time value of money defined by profit*' which is justified, real and natural.

The fact is, 'time value of money' in itself is nothing; it depends only as how you define it. This is same like time is neither good nor bad but it is the circumstances which define a good time or a bad time. It is a dilemma of competing doctrines that when a query is originated from one, naturally it uses the concepts and practices prevalent in its own belief system but when responding minds are not clear about the philosophical lacking of the querying minds then the query is not answered at a level where the answer can be justified. In case of 'time value of money' - the difference is in the definition.

About First Increase

There are few Islamic finance practitioners who are unable to see beyond financial equivalence of two debts and since they too have no answer to the conventional query or objection, and perhaps self convinced too in the matter of first increase or aggressive in responding to the query to bring a resolve; have taken this position as meant by the query. But the matter of fact is that, no argument of justification is offered by them to support this claim and position. Why first increase is justified and not the subsequent ones. Some technical reason should have been provided but there is none.

In our economic thinking, it is not mere a matter of first or subsequent increases in the contract of lending but the justification of any increase, in lending or trade. There has been extensive explanation, throughout the script, on the subject of a gain, increase or profit in any transaction. This particular query has already been answered while responding to first variant of the query 'in sales context'. In my view there is nothing left in previous answer to add here for this query. However to review, the answer is – any increase in any transaction, if it does not conform to the natural law of profit, in not justified and is illegal. It is not a matter of first or other increases in a contract whatsoever.

Of Intrinsic Utility

Not only the conventional minds but some Islamic minds are also not clear on the matter of two debts. It is true at times when Islamic legal minds try to answer conceptual queries then they end up in adding further mystification to the subject, primarily because they are not trained in 'the reason of law' domain. In fact, this variant of query is derived from the answer to original conventional query on the subject.

It is not an issue of debts only but the issue includes gains built in these debts as well. Therefore the inquiry is related to the process of the creation of debts, where the reason of distinctiveness shall exist. The reason of intrinsic value has already been dismissed by majority of Islamic intelligentsia in very convincing way. In our economic thinking as well, the distinctive reason is the legitimacy and illegality of gain (i.e., profit conforming, and interest not conforming to the natural law of profit that defines the legal status of the gains). In view of the fact that since the variant of query has no valid answer to the primary query, therefore this variant of the query is shelved on grounds that the query is not original and the answer to original query is already offered.

•••

Conclusions

We had an extremely difficult challenge to conceive any rational and convincing distinction in two gains or transactions i.e., in Islamic *Murabaha* financing and the conventional Lending on Interest transactions, because otherwise the two dealings appear very similar in their financial outlooks. Though, the experts and advocates from both doctrines have defensive positions but these stances are not supported with credible arguments and convincing reasoning therefore the dispute is still alive. The task was challenging because we had to establish some arguments based on 'so far out of sight reasons' if to resolve the query. There were no reasons available in the field of finance rather the dispute has its origin in it as stated above for their analogous financial outlooks. Logically therefore, the search was extended to deeper levels than the field of finance i.e., its source discipline of economics or further deep into the social sciences.

Only an argument can win over an argument, it has been attempted all over this discourse to bring forward arguments based on natural, conceptual and technical reasoning that may convince or help in understanding the differences between Islamic *Murabaha* Financing (*cost plus*) and conventional lending (*principal or loan plus*) transactions. The differences are philosophical in nature and the arguments are very simple to recognize.

The exchange-event is a bilateral transfer of similar or dissimilar kind of exchangeable things, or you can say it is a combination of two unilateral transfers where each transfer makes half of the transaction. The prime queries are bringing up just *fractional* or *one-sided views* of disputed transactions i.e., the lender-side view and the seller or Islamic financier-side view from respective transactions, each *one-sided view* was referring to one unilateral transfer or just half of relevant transaction. The *holistic views* of both transactions were missing. The missing parts include the unilateral transfer views from the borrower-side as well as from the buyer-side in respective transactions. The *missing fractional views* were essential study areas in two transactions under question, to find the answer.

Two *one-sided views*, comprising unilateral transfers of money only, are the basic reason for similar financial outlooks of two transactions. However, such judgment of similarity is not a justified comparison because there are at least four unilateral transfers in two transactions and the other two are not included while comparing. It may sound going in to minute details but it was needed as the issue is demanding. When included the *missing fractional views* i.e., remaining two unilateral transfers, where one is money and the other is non-money thing, then the issue no more remained a financial situation rather the inclusion pulled the matter one level up to the discipline of economics.

Though, we could have explored the answers inside the field of economics without going into above reasons since finance is sub-field of economics; however it was essential to forestall anti-arguments to flood back from already known stances. In fact, economics was natural field to search any distinction since *any gain* itself is no less than a social subject even if through a mutual affair because each individual economy is a part of societal economy. The arguments of economic distinctions are:

Since, gain comes from the counterpart in a mutual or societal affair, therefore firstly, it must exist with the counterpart and neither he nor the society shall go in to a deficient state by this transfer from him, secondly the person shall willingly be ready to deliver it at his free will, we had a litmus test of options in this regard.

The profit (gain) must conform to the natural law of profit for its technical availability and legal standing; if it does not then the profit (gain) is artificial and illegal.

The *Interest* as gain and the 'lending on interest' as a transaction does not meet above economic parameters or tests whereas *Profit* as gain and *Murabaha* financing as a transaction fulfills the conditions. Thus, two gains and the transactions under scrutiny are not similar for their economic traits and legal structure and standing.

*** End ***